2018 EMNLP Workshop SCAI: 2nd International Workshop on Search-Oriented Conversational AI

Brussels, Belgium
31 October 2018

ISBN: 978-1-5108-7425-1

EMNLP 2018

Search-Oriented Conversational AI (SCAI)

**Proceedings of the 2018 EMNLP Workshop SCAI:
The 2nd International Workshop on
Search-Oriented Conversational AI**

October 31, 2018
Brussels, Belgium

Gold Sponsors

facebook

Silver Sponsor

Bronze Sponsor

Machine Intelligence for People and Jobs

Order copies of this and other ACL proceedings from:

Association for Computational Linguistics (ACL)
209 N. Eighth Street
Stroudsburg, PA 18360
USA
Tel: +1-570-476-8006
Fax: +1-570-476-0860
acl@aclweb.org

Introduction

Welcome to the the 2nd International Workshop on Search-Oriented Conversational AI. Following the successful first edition co-located with the International Conference on the Theory of Information Retrieval (ICTIR 2017), we decided to run this workshop again, this time at an NLP conference, with the aim to bring together researchers from NLP, Machine Learning, and IR communities to instigate future direction of search-oriented conversational systems.

This year we received 22 valid submissions and decided to accept 6 papers for oral presentation and 7 papers for posters. That yields an acceptance rate of 27% for oral presentations and 59% total acceptance rate. We hope that by accepting more papers we will have more lively discussions. We are thankful to the program committee for their hard work. A separate thanks goes to the additional reviewers helping with the last-minute reviews and the PC chairs finalizing the decisions.

Aleksandr Chuklin, Jeff Dalton, Julia Kiseleva, Alexey Borisov, and Mikhail Burtsev

Organizers:

Aleksandr Chuklin, Google Zürich
Jeff Dalton, University of Glasgow
Julia Kiseleva, University of Amsterdam
Alexey Borisov, Yandex & University of Amsterdam
Mikhail Burtsev, MIPT

Steering Committee:

Joelle Pineau, McGill University
Michel Galley, Microsoft Research
Maarten de Rijke, University of Amsterdam

Program Committee:

Damiano Spina, RMIT University (Australia)
Igor Shalyminov, Heriot-Watt University (UK)
Jaap Kamps, University of Amsterdam (The Netherlands)
Tom Kenter, Google London (UK)
Valentin Malykh, MIPT (Russia)
Evgeny Kharitonov, Facebook Paris (France)
Scott Roy, Google Mountain View (USA)

Additional Reviewers:

Guillermo Garrido, Google Zürich (Switzerland)
Sascha Rothe, Google Zürich (Switzerland)

Invited Speakers:

Milica Gašić, University of Cambridge
Mari Ostendorf, University of Washington
Antoine Bordes, Facebook Research
Yun-Nung (Vivian) Chen, National Taiwan University

Table of Contents

Workshop Program

Wednesday, October 31, 2018

09:00–09:10 *Introduction*

Session 1

09:10–09:50 *Keynote 1: Antoine Bordes*

09:50–10:10 *Neural Response Ranking for Social Conversation: A Data-Efficient Approach*
Igor Shalyminov, Ondřej Dušek and Oliver Lemon

10:10–10:30 *Autonomous Sub-domain Modeling for Dialogue Policy with Hierarchical Deep Reinforcement Learning*
Giovanni Yoko Kristianto, Huiwen Zhang, Bin Tong, Makoto Iwayama and Yoshiyuki Kobayashi

10:30–11:00 *Break*

Session 2

11:00–11:40 *Keynote 2: Milica Gašić*

11:40–12:00 *Building Dialogue Structure from Discourse Tree of a Question*
Boris Galitsky and Dmitry Ilvovsky

12:00–12:20 *A Methodology for Evaluating Interaction Strategies of Task-Oriented Conversational Agents*
Marco Guerini, Sara Falcone and Bernardo Magnini

12:20–12:40 *A Reinforcement Learning-driven Translation Model for Search-Oriented Conversational Systems*
Wafa Aissa, Laure Soulier and Ludovic Denoyer

12:40–14:00 *Lunch*

Session 3

14:00–14:40   *Keynote 3: Yun-Nung (Vivian) Chen*

14:40–15:00   *Research Challenges in Building a Voice-based Artificial Personal Shopper - Position Paper*
Nut Limsopatham, Oleg Rokhlenko and David Carmel

15:00–15:30   *Poster session*

15:30–16:00   *Break*

Session 4

16:00–16:40   *Keynote 4: Mari Ostendorf*

16:40–17:20   *Roundtable discussion*

17:20–17:30   *Closing*

Neural Response Ranking for Social Conversation:
A Data-Efficient Approach

Igor Shalyminov, Ondřej Dušek, and Oliver Lemon
The Interaction Lab, Department of Computer Science
Heriot-Watt University, Edinburgh, EH14 4AS, UK
{is33, o.dusek, o.lemon}@hw.ac.uk

Abstract

The overall objective of 'social' dialogue systems is to support engaging, entertaining, and lengthy conversations on a wide variety of topics, including social chit-chat. Apart from raw dialogue data, user-provided ratings are the most common signal used to train such systems to produce engaging responses. In this paper we show that social dialogue systems can be trained effectively from raw unannotated data. Using a dataset of real conversations collected in the 2017 Alexa Prize challenge, we developed a neural ranker[1] for selecting 'good' system responses to user utterances, i.e. responses which are likely to lead to long and engaging conversations. We show that (1) our neural ranker consistently outperforms several strong baselines when trained to optimise for user ratings; (2) when trained on larger amounts of data and only using conversation length as the objective, the ranker performs better than the one trained using ratings – ultimately reaching a Precision@1 of 0.87. This advance will make data collection for social conversational agents simpler and less expensive in the future.

1 Introduction

Chatbots, or *socialbots*, are dialogue systems aimed at maintaining an open-domain conversation with the user spanning a wide range of topics, with the main objective of being engaging, entertaining, and natural. Under one of the current approaches to such systems, the *bot ensemble* (Serban et al., 2017; Yu et al., 2016; Song et al., 2016), a collection, or ensemble, of different bots is used, each of which proposes a candidate response to the user's input, and a *response ranker* selects the best response for the final system output to be uttered to the user.

In this paper, we focus on the task of finding the best supervision signal for training a response ranker for ensemble systems. Our contribution is twofold: first, we present a neural ranker for ensemble-based dialogue systems and evaluate its level of performance using an annotation type which is often used in open-domain dialogue and was provided to the Alexa Prize 2017 participants by Amazon (Ram et al., 2017): per-dialogue user ratings. Second and most importantly, we explore an alternative way of assessing social conversations simply via their *length*, thus removing the need for any user-provided ratings.

2 Data Efficiency in Social Dialogue

2.1 The Need for Data Efficiency

It is well known that deep learning models are highly data-dependent, but there are currently no openly available data sources which can provide enough high-quality open-domain social dialogues for building a production-level socialbot. Therefore, a common way to get the necessary data is to collect it on a crowdsourcing platform (Krause et al., 2017). Based on the model type and the development stage, it may be necessary to collect either whole dialogues, or some form of human feedback on how good a particular dialogue or turn is. However, both kinds of data are time-consuming and expensive to collect.

The data efficiency of a dialogue model can be split into two parts accordingly:

- *sample efficiency* – the number of data points needed for the model to train. As such, it is useful to specify an order of magnitude of the training set size for different types of machine learning models;
- *annotation efficiency* – the amount of annotation

---

[1]Code and trained models are available at https://github.com/WattSocialBot/alana_learning_to_rank

1

Proceedings of the 2018 EMNLP Workshop SCAI: The 2nd Int'l Workshop on Search-Oriented Conversational AI, pages 1–8
Brussels, Belgium, October 31, 2018. ©2018 Association for Computational Linguistics

Variables	Pearson corr. coefficient
rating/length	0.11
rating/positive feedback	0.11
rating/negative feedback	0.04
length/positive feedback	0.67
length/negative feedback	0.49

Table 1: Correlation study of key dialogue aspects

effort needed. For instance, traditional goal-oriented dialogue system architectures normally require *intent*, *slot value*, and *dialogue state* annotation (e.g. Young et al., 2010), whereas end-to-end conversational models work simply with raw text transcriptions (e.g. Vinyals and Le, 2015).

2.2 Alexa Prize Ratings

The 2017 Alexa Prize challenge made it possible to collect large numbers of dialogues between real users of Amazon Echo devices and various chatbots. The only annotation collected was per-dialogue ratings elicited at the end of conversations by asking the user *"On a scale of 1 to 5, how much would you like to speak with this bot again"* (Venkatesh et al., 2017). Less than 50% of conversations were actually rated; the rest were quit without the user giving a score. In addition, note that a single rating is applied to an entire conversation (rather than individual turns), which may consist of very many utterances. The conversations in the challenge were about 2.5 minutes long on average, and about 10% of conversations were over 10 minutes long (Ram et al., 2017) – this makes the ratings very sparse. Finally, the ratings are noisy – some dialogues which are clearly bad can get good ratings from some users, and vice-versa.

Given the main objective of social dialogue stated in the Alexa Prize rules as 'long and engaging' conversation, we tried to verify an assumption that user ratings reflect these properties of the dialogue. Apart from our observations above, we performed a correlation analysis of user ratings and aspects of dialogue directly reflecting the objective: dialogue length and explicit user feedback (see Table 1).

Although we have a significant number of dialogues which are both long and highly rated, the correlation analysis was not able to show any relationship between dialogue length and rating. Neither are ratings correlated with user feedback (see Section 6 for the details of user feedback collection). On the other hand, we found a promis-

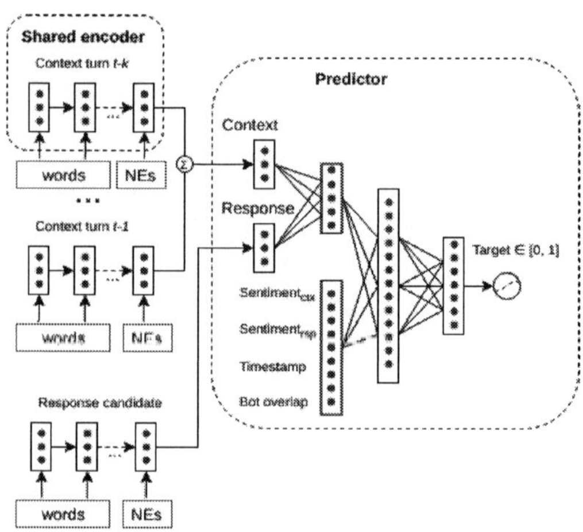

Figure 1: Neural ranker architecture

ing moderate correlation between the conversation length and explicit positive feedback from users (specifically, the number of dialogue turns containing it). The respective length/negative feedback relationship is slightly weaker.

Therefore, we experiment with conversation length for approximating user satisfaction and engagement and use it as an alternative measure of dialogue quality. This allows us to take advantage of all conversations, not just those rated by users, for training a ranker. While some conversations might be long but not engaging (e.g. if there are a lot of misunderstandings, corrections, and speech recognition errors), training a ranker only using length makes it extremely *annotation-efficient*.

3 A neural ranker for open-domain conversation

The ranker described here is part of Alana, Heriot-Watt University's Alexa Prize 2017 finalist socialbot (Papaioannou et al., 2017). Alana is an ensemble-based model incorporating information-retrieval-based bots with news content and information on a wide range of topics from Wikipedia, a question answering system, and rule-based bots for various purposes, from amusing users with fun facts to providing a consistent persona. The rule-based bots are also required to handle sensitive issues which can be raised by real users, such as medical, financial, and legal advice, as well as profanities.

3.1 Ranker architecture

The architecture of our ranker is shown in Figure 1. The inputs to the model are 1-hot vectors of a candidate response and the current dialogue context (we use the 3 most recent system and user turns). They are encoded into a latent representation using a single shared RNN encoder based on GRU cells (Cho et al., 2014). The context embedding vectors are then summed up and concatenated with the response embedding (Eq. 1):

$$Enc(C, r) = \sum_i RNN(C_i) \oplus RNN(r) \quad (1)$$

where C is the dialogue context and r is a response candidate.

The context and the response are represented using combined word-agent tokens (where agent is either a specific bot from the ensemble or the user) and are concatenated with the lists of named entities extracted using Stanford NER (Finkel et al., 2005). All the word-agent tokens and named entities share the same unified vocabulary.

Encoder outputs, along with additional dialogue features such as context and response sentiment, timestamp, and bot names in the context and the response, go into the *Predictor*, a feed-forward neural network (MLP) whose output is the resulting rating (Eq. 2):

$$Pred(C, r) = \sigma(L(Sem(C, r) \oplus f(C, r))) \quad (2)$$

where: $L(x) = ReLU(Mx + b)$ is the layer used in the Predictor (the number of such layers is a model parameter),
$Sem = L(Enc(C, r))$ is the vector of semantic context-response features, and
$f(C, r)$ is a vector of the additional dialogue features listed above.

We use $ReLU$ activation for the hidden layers because it is known to be highly efficient with deep architectures (Glorot et al., 2011). Finally, we use sigmoid activation σ for generating the final prediction in the range $[0, 1]$.

3.2 Training method

We use either dialogue rating or length as the prediction target (as discussed in Sections 5 and 6). The model is trained to minimize the Mean Squared Error (MSE) loss against the target using the Adagrad optimizer (Duchi et al., 2011). In our training setup, the model learns to predict per-turn target values. However, since only per-dialogue ones are available in the data, we use the following approximation: the target value of a context-response pair is the target value of the dialogue containing it. The intuition behind this is an assumption that the majority of turns in "good" dialogues (either length- or rating-wise) are "good" in their local contexts as well – so that given a large number of dialogues, the most successful and unsuccessful turns will emerge from the corresponding dialogues.

4 Baselines

We compare our neural ranker to two other models also developed during the competition: *handcrafted* and *linear* rankers — all three were deployed live in the Alana Alexa Prize 2017 finalist system (Papaioannou et al., 2017), and were therefore of sufficient quality for a production system receiving thousands of calls per day. We also compare our model to a recently published *dual-encoder* response selection model by Lu et al. (2017) based on an approach principally close to ours.

4.1 Handcrafted ranker

In the handcrafted approach, several turn-level and dialogue-level features are calculated, and a linear combination of those feature values with manually adjusted coefficients is used to predict the final ranking. The list of features includes:

- coherence, information flow, and dullness as defined by Li et al. (2016);
- overlap between the context and the response with regards to named entities and noun phrases;
- topic divergence between the context turns and the response – topics are represented using the *Latent Dirichlet Allocation* (LDA) model (Hoffman et al., 2010);
- sentiment polarity, as computed by the NLTK Vader sentiment analyser (Gilbert and Hutto, 2014).[2]

4.2 Linear ranker

The linear ranker is based on the VowpalWabbit (VW) linear model (Agarwal et al., 2014). We use

---

[2] http://www.nltk.org/howto/sentiment.html

the MSE loss function and the following features in our VW ranker model:

- bag-of-n-grams from the dialogue context (preceding 3 utterances) and the response,
- position-specific n-grams at the beginning of the context and the response (first 5 positions),
- dialogue flow features (Li et al., 2016), the same as for the handcrafted ranker,
- bot name, from the set of bots in the ensemble.

4.3 Dual-encoder ranker

The closest architecture to our neural ranker is that of (Lu et al., 2017), who use a dual-encoder LSTM with a predictor MLP for task-oriented dialogue in closed domains. Unlike this work, they do not use named entities, sentiment, or other input features than basic word embeddings. Dialogue context is not modelled explicitly either, and is limited to a single user turn. We reproduced their architecture and set its parameters to the best ones reported in the original paper.

5 Training data

Our data is transcripts of conversations between our socialbot and real users of the Amazon Echo collected over the challenge period, February–December 2017. The dataset consists of over 200,000 dialogues (5,000,000+ turns) from which over 100,000 dialogues (totalling nearly 3,000,000 turns) are annotated with ratings. From this data, we sampled two datasets of matching size for training our rankers, using the per-turn target value approximation described in Section 3.2 – the *Length* and *Rating* datasets for the respective versions of rankers.

The target values (length/rating) in both sets are normalized into the $[0, 1]$ range, and the *Length* set contains context-response pairs from long dialogues (target value above 0.7) as positive instances and context-response pairs from short dialogues (target value below 0.3) as negative ones. With the same selection criteria, the *Rating* set contains context-response pairs from highly rated dialogues (ratings 4 and 5) as positive instances and context-response pairs from low-rated dialogues (ratings 1 and 2) as negative ones. Both datasets contain 500,000 instances in total, with equal proportion of positive and negative instances. We use a 8:1:1 split for training, development, and test sets.

Prior to creating both datasets, we filtered out of the dialogue transcripts all system turns which cannot be treated as natural social interaction (e.g. a quiz game) as well as outliers (interaction length $\geq$ 95th percentile or less than 3 turns long).[3] Thresholds of 0.3 and 0.7 were set heuristically based on preliminary data analysis. On the one hand, these values provide contrastive-enough ratings (e.g. we are not sure whether the rating in the middle of the scale can be interpreted as negative or positive). On the other hand, they allow us to get enough training data for both Length and Rating datasets.[4]

6 Evaluation and experimental setup

In order to tune the neural rankers, we performed a grid search over the shared encoder GRU layer size and the Predictor topology.[5] The best configurations are determined by the loss on the development sets. For evaluation, we used an independent dataset.

6.1 Evaluation based on explicit user feedback

At the evaluation stage, we check how well the rankers can distinguish between good responses and bad ones. The criterion for 'goodness' that we use here is chosen to be independent from both training signals. Specifically, we collected an evaluation set composed of dialogue turns followed by explicit user feedback, e.g. "great, thank you", "that was interesting" (we refer to it as the *User feedback* dataset). Our 'bad' response candidates are randomly sampled across the dataset.

The user feedback turns were identified using sentiment analysis in combination with a whitelist and a blacklist of hand-picked phrases, so that in total we used 605 unique utterances, e.g. *"that's pretty cool"*, *"you're funny"*, *"gee thanks"*, *"interesting fact"*, *"funny alexa you're funny"*.

'Goodness' defined in this way allows us to evaluate how well our two approximated training signals can optimize for the user's satisfaction as explicitly expressed at the turn level, thus leading

---

[3]Some extremely long dialogues are due to users repeating themselves over and over, and so this filter removes these bad dialogues from the dataset. Dialogues less than 3 turns long are often where the user accidentally triggered the chatbot. These outliers amounted to about 14% of our data.

[4]Using more extreme thresholds did not produce enough data while less ones did not provide adequate training signal.

[5]We tested GRU sizes of 64, 128, 256 and Predictor layers number/sizes of [128], [128, 64], [128, 32, 32].

to our desired behaviour, i.e., producing long and engaging dialogues.

The *User feedback* dataset contains 24,982 $\langle context, good\_response, bad\_response \rangle$ tuples in total.

To evaluate the rankers on this dataset, we use *precision@k*, which is commonly used for information retrieval system evaluation (Eq. 3).

$$P@k(c, R) = \frac{\sum_{i=1}^{k} Relevant(c, R_k)}{k} \qquad (3)$$

where c is dialogue context, R is response candidates list, and $Relevant$ is a binary predicate indicating whether a particular response is relevant to the context.

Precision is typically used together with recall and F-measure. However, since our dialogue data is extremely sparse so that it is hard to find multiple good responses for the same exact dialogue context, recall and F-measure cannot be applied to this setting. Therefore, since we only perform pairwise ranking, we use *precision@1* to check that the good answer is the top-ranked one. Also due to data sparsity, we only perform this evaluation with *gold positive* responses and *sampled negative* ones – it is typically not possible to find a good response with exactly the same context as a given bad response.

6.2 Interim results

The results of our first experiment are shown in Table 2. We can see that the neural ranker trained with user ratings clearly outperforms all the alternative approaches in terms of test set loss on its respective dataset as well as pairwise ranking precision on the evaluation dataset. Also note that both versions of the neural ranker stand extremely close to each other on both evaluation criteria, given a much greater gap between them and their next-best-performing alternatives, the linear rankers.

The dual-encoder ranker turned out to be not an efficient model for our problem, partly because it was originally optimized for a different task as reported by Lu et al. (2017).

7 Training on larger amounts of data

A major advantage of training on raw dialogue transcripts is data volume: in our case, we have roughly twice as many raw dialogues as rated ones (cf. Section 5). This situation is very common in

Model	P@1 (eval set)	Loss (test set)
Handcrafted	0.478	—
VowpalWabbit@length	0.742	0.199
VowpalWabbit@rating	0.773	0.202
DualEncoder@length	0.365	0.239
DualEncoder@rating	0.584	0.247
Neural@length	0.824	0.139
Neural@rating	**0.847**	**0.138**

Table 2: Ranking models evaluation: pairwise ranking precision on the independent *User feedback* dataset and loss on the *Length/Rating* test sets (Section 5) for the corresponding trainset sizes of 500,000.

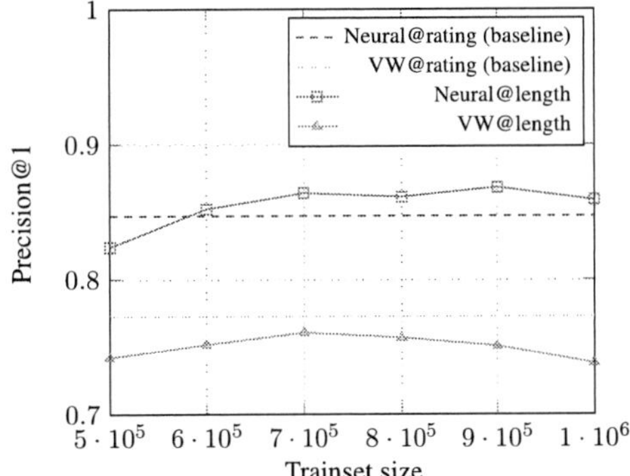

Figure 2: Comparison of rankers trained on extended datasets

data-driven development: since data annotation is a very expensive and slow procedure, almost always there is significantly more raw data than annotated data of a high quality. To illustrate this, we collected extended training datasets of raw dialogues of up to 1,000,000 data points for training from the length signal. We trained our neural ranker and the VW ranker using the same configuration as in Section 6.[6]

The results are shown in Figure 2, where we see that the neural ranker trained on the length signal consistently outperform the ratings-based one. Its trend, although fluctuating, is more stable than that of VW – we believe that this is due to VW's inherent lower model capacity as well as its training setup, which is mainly optimised for speed. The figure also shows that VW@length is worse than VW@rating, regardless of training data size.

8 Discussion and future work

Our evaluation results show that the neural ranker presented above is an efficient approach to re-

---

[6]We were not able to train the dual encoder ranker on all the extended datasets due to the time constraints.

sponse ranking for social conversation. On a medium-sized training set, the two versions of the neural ranker, length and ratings-based, showed strongly superior performance to three alternative ranking approaches, and performed competitively with each other. Furthermore, the experiment with extended training sets shows that the accuracy of the length-based neural ranker grows steadily given more unannotated training data, outperforming the rating-based ranker with only slightly larger training sets.

The overall results of our experiments confirm that dialogue length, even approximated in quite a straightforward way, provides a sufficient supervision signal for training a ranker for a social conversation model. In future work, we will attempt to further improve the model using the same data in an adversarial setup following Wang et al. (2017). We also plan to directly train our model for pairwise ranking in the fashion of Burges et al. (2005) instead of the current pointwise approach. Finally, we are going to employ contextual sampling of negative responses using approximate nearest neighbour search (Johnson et al., 2017) in order to perform a more efficient pairwise training.

9 Related work

Work on response ranking for conversational systems has been been growing rapidly in recent years. Some authors employ ranking based on heuristically defined measures: Yu et al. (2015, 2016) use a heuristic based on keyword matching, part-of-speech filters, and Word2Vec similarity. (Krause et al., 2017) apply standard information retrieval metrics (TF-IDF) with importance weighting for named entities. However, most of the recent research attempts to train the ranking function from large amounts of conversational data, as we do. Some authors use task-based conversations, such as IT forums (Lowe et al., 2015) or customer services (Lu et al., 2017; Kumar et al., 2018), while others focus on online conversations on social media (e.g. Wu et al., 2016; Al-Rfou et al., 2016).

The basic approach to learning the ranking function in most recent work is the same (e.g. Lowe et al., 2015; Al-Rfou et al., 2016; Wu et al., 2016): the predictor is taught to rank positive responses taken from real dialogue data higher than randomly sampled negative examples. Some of the approaches do not even include rich dialogue contexts and use only immediate context-response pairs for ranking (Ji et al., 2014; Yan et al., 2016; Lu et al., 2017). Some authors improve upon this basic scenario: Zhuang et al. (2018) take a desired emotion of the response into account; Liu et al. (2017) focus on the engagement of responses based on Reddit comments rating; Fedorenko et al. (2017) train the ranking model in several iterations, using highly ranked incorrect responses as negative examples for the next iteration. Nevertheless, to our knowledge, none of the prior works attempt to optimise for long-term dialogue quality; unlike in our work, their only ranking criterion is focused on the immediate response.

10 Conclusion

We have presented a neural response ranker for open-domain 'social' dialogue systems and described two methods for training it using common supervision signals coming from conversational data: user-provided ratings and dialogue length. We demonstrated its efficiency by evaluating it using explicit positive feedback as a measure for user engagement. Specifically, trained on ratings, our neural ranker consistently outperforms several strong baselines; moreover, given larger amounts of data and only using conversation length as the objective, the ranker performs better the ratings-based one, reaching 0.87 Precision@1. This shows that conversation length can be used as an optimisation objective for generating engaging social dialogues, which means that we no longer need the expensive and time-consuming procedure of collecting per-dialogue user ratings, as was done for example in the Alexa Prize 2017 and is common practice in conversational AI research. Per-turn user ratings may still be valuable to collect for such systems, but these are even more expensive and problematic to obtain. Looking ahead, this advance will make data collection for social conversational agents simpler and less expensive in the future.

Acknowledgements

This research received funding from the EPSRC project MaDrIgAL (EP/N017536/1). The Titan Xp used for this research was donated by the NVIDIA Corporation.

References

Alekh Agarwal, Olivier Chapelle, Miroslav Dudík, and John Langford. 2014. A reliable effective terascale linear learning system. *Journal of Machine Learning Research*, 15(1):1111–1133.

Rami Al-Rfou, Marc Pickett, Javier Snaider, Yunhsuan Sung, Brian Strope, and Ray Kurzweil. 2016. Conversational Contextual Cues: The Case of Personalization and History for Response Ranking. *CoRR*, abs/1606.00372.

Christopher J. C. Burges, Tal Shaked, Erin Renshaw, Ari Lazier, Matt Deeds, Nicole Hamilton, and Gregory N. Hullender. 2005. Learning to rank using gradient descent. In *Proceedings of ICML*, pages 89–96.

Kyunghyun Cho, Bart van Merriënboer, Çağlar Gülçehre, Dzmitry Bahdanau, Fethi Bougares, Holger Schwenk, and Yoshua Bengio. 2014. Learning phrase representations using rnn encoder–decoder for statistical machine translation. In *Proceedings of the 2014 Conference on Empirical Methods in Natural Language Processing (EMNLP)*, pages 1724–1734, Doha, Qatar.

John C. Duchi, Elad Hazan, and Yoram Singer. 2011. Adaptive subgradient methods for online learning and stochastic optimization. *Journal of Machine Learning Research*, 12:2121–2159.

Denis Fedorenko, Nikita Smetanin, and Artem Rodichev. 2017. Avoiding Echo-Responses in a Retrieval-Based Conversation System. *CoRR*, abs/1712.05626.

Jenny Rose Finkel, Trond Grenager, and Christopher D. Manning. 2005. Incorporating non-local information into information extraction systems by gibbs sampling. In *Proceedings of ACL*, pages 363–370.

C. J. Gilbert and Erric Hutto. 2014. VADER: A parsimonious rule-based model for sentiment analysis of social media text. In *Eighth International AAAI Conference on Weblogs and Social Media*, pages 216–225, Ann Arbor, MI, USA.

Xavier Glorot, Antoine Bordes, and Yoshua Bengio. 2011. Deep sparse rectifier neural networks. In *Proceedings of AISTATS*, pages 315–323.

Matthew Hoffman, Francis R. Bach, and David M. Blei. 2010. Online learning for latent dirichlet allocation. In J. D. Lafferty, C. K. I. Williams, J. Shawe-Taylor, R. S. Zemel, and A. Culotta, editors, *Advances in Neural Information Processing Systems 23*, pages 856–864.

Zongcheng Ji, Zhengdong Lu, and Hang Li. 2014. An Information Retrieval Approach to Short Text Conversation. *CoRR*, abs/1408.6988.

Jeff Johnson, Matthijs Douze, and Hervé Jégou. 2017. Billion-scale similarity search with GPUs. *CoRR*, abs/1702.08734.

Ben Krause, Marco Damonte, Mihai Dobre, Daniel Duma, Joachim Fainberg, Federico Fancellu, Emmanuel Kahembwe, Jianpeng Cheng, and Bonnie Webber. 2017. Edina: Building an Open Domain Socialbot with Self-dialogues. In *1st Proceedings of Alexa Prize*, Las Vegas, NV, USA. ArXiv: 1709.09816.

Girish Kumar, Matthew Henderson, Shannon Chan, Hoang Nguyen, and Lucas Ngoo. 2018. Question-Answer Selection in User to User Marketplace Conversations. *CoRR*, abs/1802.01766.

Jiwei Li, Will Monroe, Alan Ritter, Michel Galley, Jianfeng Gao, and Dan Jurafsky. 2016. Deep Reinforcement Learning for Dialogue Generation. In *Proc. EMNLP*, pages 1192–1202.

Huiting Liu, Tao Lin, Hanfei Sun, Weijian Lin, Chih-Wei Chang, Teng Zhong, and Alexander Rudnicky. 2017. RubyStar: A Non-Task-Oriented Mixture Model Dialog System. In *1st Proceedings of Alexa Prize*, Las Vegas, NV, USA. ArXiv: 1711.02781.

Ryan Lowe, Nissan Pow, Iulian Serban, and Joelle Pineau. 2015. The Ubuntu dialogue corpus: A large dataset for research in unstructured multi-turn dialogue systems. In *Proceedings of SIGDIAL*, pages 285–294.

Yichao Lu, Phillip Keung, Shaonan Zhang, Jason Sun, and Vikas Bhardwaj. 2017. A practical approach to dialogue response generation in closed domains. *CoRR*, abs/1703.09439.

Ioannis Papaioannou, Amanda Cercas Curry, Jose L. Part, Igor Shalyminov, Xinnuo Xu, Yanchao Yu, Ondrej Dusek, Verena Rieser, and Oliver Lemon. 2017. An ensemble model with ranking for social dialogue. In *NIPS Workshop on Conversational AI*.

Ashwin Ram, Rohit Prasad, Chandra Khatri, Anu Venkatesh, Raefer Gabriel, Qing Liu, Jeff Nunn, Behnam Hedayatnia, Ming Cheng, Ashish Nagar, Eric King, Kate Bland, Amanda Wartick, Yi Pan, Han Song, Sk Jayadevan, Gene Hwang, and Art Pettigrue. 2017. Conversational AI: The Science Behind the Alexa Prize. In *1st Proceedings of Alexa Prize*, Las Vegas, NV, USA. ArXiv: 1801.03604.

Iulian Vlad Serban, Chinnadhurai Sankar, Mathieu Germain, Saizheng Zhang, Zhouhan Lin, Sandeep Subramanian, Taesup Kim, Michael Pieper, Sarath Chandar, Nan Rosemary Ke, Sai Mudumba, Alexandre de Brébisson, Jose Sotelo, Dendi Suhubdy, Vincent Michalski, Alexandre Nguyen, Joelle Pineau, and Yoshua Bengio. 2017. A deep reinforcement learning chatbot. *NIPS Workshop on Conversational AI*, abs/1709.02349.

Yiping Song, Rui Yan, Xiang Li, Dongyan Zhao, and Ming Zhang. 2016. Two are better than one: An ensemble of retrieval- and generation-based dialog systems. *CoRR*, abs/1610.07149.

Anu Venkatesh, Chandra Khatri, Ashwin Ram, Fenfei Guo, Raefer Gabriel, Ashish Nagar, Rohit Prasad, Ming Cheng, Behnam Hedayatnia, Angeliki Metallinou, Rahul Goel, Shaohua Yang, and Anirudh Raju. 2017. On Evaluating and Comparing Conversational Agents. In *NIPS 2017 Workshop on Conversational AI (ConvAI)*, Long Beach, CA, USA. ArXiv: 1801.03625.

Oriol Vinyals and Quoc V. Le. 2015. A neural conversational model. *ICML Deep Learning Workshop 2015*.

Jun Wang, Lantao Yu, Weinan Zhang, Yu Gong, Yinghui Xu, Benyou Wang, Peng Zhang, and Dell Zhang. 2017. Irgan: A minimax game for unifying generative and discriminative information retrieval models. In *Proceedings of SIGIR*, pages 515–524, Shinjuku, Japan.

Bowen Wu, Baoxun Wang, and Hui Xue. 2016. Ranking responses oriented to conversational relevance in chat-bots. In *Proceedings of COLING*, pages 652– 662, Osaka, Japan.

Rui Yan, Yiping Song, and Hua Wu. 2016. Learning to Respond with Deep Neural Networks for Retrieval-Based Human-Computer Conversation System. In *Proceedings of SIGIR*, pages 55–64, Pisa, Italy.

Steve Young, Milica Gašić, Simon Keizer, François Mairesse, Jost Schatzmann, Blaise Thomson, and Kai Yu. 2010. The Hidden Information State model: A practical framework for POMDP-based spoken dialogue management. *Computer Speech & Language*, 24(2):150–174.

Zhou Yu, Alexandros Papangelis, and Alex Rudnicky. 2015. TickTock: A Non-Goal-Oriented Multimodal Dialog System with Engagement Awareness. In *Turn-Taking and Coordination in Human-Machine Interaction: Papers from the 2015 AAAI Spring Symposium*, pages 108–111, Palo Alto, CA, USA.

Zhou Yu, Ziyu Xu, Alan W Black, and Alex I. Rudnicky. 2016. Strategy and Policy Learning for Non-Task-Oriented Conversational Systems. In *Proc. SIGDIAL*, Los Angeles, CA, USA.

Yimeng Zhuang, Xianliang Wang, Han Zhang, Jinghui Xie, and Xuan Zhu. 2018. An Ensemble Approach to Conversation Generation. In *Natural Language Processing and Chinese Computing*, volume 10619, pages 51–62. Springer International Publishing. DOI: 10.1007/978-3-319-73618-1_5.

Autonomous Sub-domain Modeling for Dialogue Policy with Hierarchical Deep Reinforcement Learning

Giovanni Yoko Kristianto[1], Huiwen Zhang[2,3], Bin Tong[1],
Makoto Iwayama[1], Yoshiyuki Kobayashi[1]

[1]Hitachi Central Research Laboratory, Tokyo, Japan
[2]Shenyang Institute of Automation, Chinese Academy of Sciences, Shenyang, China
[3]University of Chinese Academy of Sciences, Beijing, China
{*yokogiovanni.kristianto.oq, bin.tong.hh, makoto.iwayama.nw, yoshiyuki.kobayashi.gp*} *@hitachi.com*
zhanghuiwen@sia.cn

Abstract

Solving composites tasks, which consist of several inherent sub-tasks, remains a challenge in the research area of dialogue. Current studies have tackled this issue by manually decomposing the composite tasks into several sub-domains. However, much human effort is inevitable. This paper proposes a dialogue framework that autonomously models meaningful sub-domains and learns the policy over them. Our experiments show that our framework outperforms the baseline without sub-domains by 11% in terms of success rate, and is competitive with that with manually defined sub-domains.

1 Introduction

Modeling a composite dialogue (Peng et al., 2017), which consists of several inherent sub-tasks, is in high demand due to the complexity of human conversation. For instance, a composite dialogue of making a hotel reservation involves several sub-tasks, such as looking for a hotel that meets the user's constraints, booking the room, and paying for the room. The completion of a composite dialogue requires the fulfillment of all involved sub-tasks. In this paper, we focus on the development of a dialogue agent that can discover inherent sub-tasks autonomously from a composite domain, learn a policy to fulfill each sub-task, and learn a policy among these sub-tasks to solve the composite task. Composite dialogues are different from multi-domain dialogues. In multi-domain dialogue systems (Cuayáhuitl et al., 2016; Gasic et al., 2016), each dialogue typically involves one domain, and consequently, its fulfillment does not need policy across domains.

To develop a dialogue agent that can handle a composite task, using standard flat reinforcement learning (RL), which are often used for dialogues with a simple task (Young et al., 2013; Gašić and Young, 2014; Williams et al., 2017; Casanueva et al., 2017; Li et al., 2017), might be inappropriate. Flat RL methods, such as DQN (Mnih et al., 2015), could suffer from the curse of dimensionality, that is the number of parameters to be learned grows exponentially with the size of any compact encoding of system state. Therefore, flat RL is unable to learn reliable value functions (Kulkarni et al., 2016) for a composite task. A composite task has a larger state space and action set, longer trajectory, and more sparse rewards than a simple task. Hierarchical reinforcement learning (HRL) (Dietterich, 2000; Parr and Russell, 1997) is a technique to model complex dialogues (Cuayáhuitl, 2009). Peng et al. (2017) and Budzianowski et al. (2017) used the options framework (Sutton et al., 1999) to solve the above problems in composite dialogues and showed its superiority over flat RL. In their work, however, each option (i.e. sub-task) and its property (e.g. starting and terminating conditions, and valid action set) had to be manually defined. Such handcrafted options ease the policy learning in a composite task, but much human effort is inevitable.

To solve the above problems, we propose to model sub-domains autonomously without any human intervention. The modeled sub-domains imitate the intentions to fulfill sub-tasks in a dialogue, which consequently can be reused by similar yet different domains. Challenges to achieve such autonomous sub-domain modeling include (i) how to discover meaningful sub-domains and their properties (i.e. starting conditions, terminating conditions, and the policies), and (ii) how to have a coherent interaction among these sub-domains so that the dialogue agent can accomplish a dialogue goal efficiently. To tackle these challenges, we propose a unified framework that integrates *option discovery* (Bacon et al., 2017; Machado et al., 2017) with HRL to learn the opti-

Proceedings of the 2018 EMNLP Workshop SCAI: The 2nd Int'l Workshop on Search-Oriented Conversational AI, pages 9–16
Brussels, Belgium, October 31, 2018. ©2018 Association for Computational Linguistics

mal policies over options. With an evaluation involving a task of reserving hotel room, we confirm that our framework achieves a significant improvement over flat RL by 11% in terms of success rate, and is competitive with the framework with manually defined options (Budzianowski et al., 2017).

2 Hierarchical Policy Management

A composite task can be decomposed into a sequence of sub-domains, which are also called options. The composite task is accomplished when all these sub-domains are fulfilled. Following the options framework (Sutton et al., 1999), our dialogue agent handles the composite task by designing two levels of policies in a hierarchical structure, as shown in Figure 1.

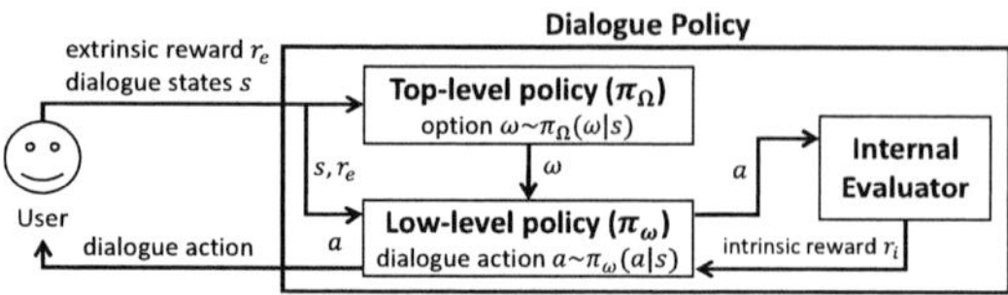

Figure 1: Overview of our dialogue policy.

In this hierarchical policy framework, $\mathcal{S}$ denotes the dialogue state space, Ω the option space, and $\mathcal{A}$ the action set. For a dialogue state $s \in \mathcal{S}$, the top-level policy π_Ω determines which option $\omega \in \Omega$ should be chosen. Then, the policy π_ω determines which primitive action $a \in \mathcal{A}$ should be chosen in option ω for s. As shown by the example in Figure 2, a primitive action is an action lasting for one time step, while an option is an action lasting several time steps. For each s, a dialogue action, which is a primitive action, is returned to the user. The dialogue system will receive an extrinsic reward r_e and a new belief state s'. An optimal policy π^* maximizes the expected discounted return $G_t = \mathbb{E}_{\pi,P}[\sum_{k=0}^{\infty} \gamma^k r_{e,t+k+1}|s_t]$ at every time step t, where P is a transition probability kernel, $\gamma \in [0,1]$ is a discount factor, and $r_{e,t'}$ is the extrinsic reward obtained at step t'.

Figure 2 shows an example of the execution of our hierarchical dialogue policy in a dialogue domain about hotel room reservation. This domain comprises two sub-domains, i.e., searching for a hotel and booking a hotel room. In this example, we assume that the dialogue system has prior knowledge regarding these sub-domains. In this paper, we propose a dialogue framework that can autonomously discover such sub-domains.

3 Autonomous Sub-Domain Modeling

An option is defined as 3-tuple $\omega = \langle \mathcal{I}_\omega, \pi_\omega, \beta_\omega \rangle$, where $\mathcal{I}_\omega \subseteq \mathcal{S}$ is the initiation set of states where ω can be chosen, $\pi_\omega : \mathcal{S} \times \mathcal{A} \rightarrow [0,1]$ is the policy of ω, and $\beta : \mathcal{S} \rightarrow [0,1]$ is the termination condition of ω. To autonomously discover options and learn their policies, we proposed to integrate option-critic (OC) (Bacon et al., 2017) and proto-value functions (PVFs) (Mahadevan, 2007; Machado et al., 2017) into a unified framework.

3.1 Option-Critic Architecture

OC is a gradient-based approach for simultaneously learning intra-option policies π_ω and termination functions β_ω. It learns options gradually from its interactions with environment. It uses option value function $Q_\Omega(s, \omega)$ defined as follows.

$$Q_\Omega(s, \omega) = \sum_a \pi_\omega(a|s) Q_U(s, \omega, a)$$

$$Q_U(s, \omega, a) = r(s, a) + \gamma \sum_{s'} P(s'|s, a) U(\omega, s')$$

$$U(\omega, s') = (1 - \beta_\omega(s')) Q_\Omega(s', \omega) + \beta_\omega(s') V_\Omega(s')$$

$Q_U(s, \omega, a)$ is the value of executing an action in the context of a state-option pair, and $U(\omega, s')$ is the utility from s' onwards, given that we arrive in s' using ω. We parameterize π_ω by θ and β_ω by ϑ. The learning algorithm of OC involves two steps:

- *options evaluation:* updating Q_Ω and Q_U with temporal difference errors; and

- *options improvement:* updating θ with $\frac{\partial Q_\Omega}{\partial \theta}$ and ϑ with $\frac{\partial Q_\Omega}{\partial \vartheta}$.

To obtain policy π_Ω over options, we combine OC with intra-option Q-learning (Sutton et al., 1999). Hereinafter, this combination is denoted as HRL-OC.

HRL-OC optimizes the options and their policies for maximizing the cumulative *extrinsic* reward. It is focused less on discovering meaningful options (Bacon et al., 2017), which may result in unnatural sub-domains in a successful conversation. To tackle this issue, we use PVFs, which are capable of capturing the geometry of the state space, to discover meaningful sub-domains.

3.2 Proto-Value Functions as Options

Proto-value functions (PVFs) are learned representations that approximate state-value function in RL (Mahadevan, 2007). Machado et al. (2017)

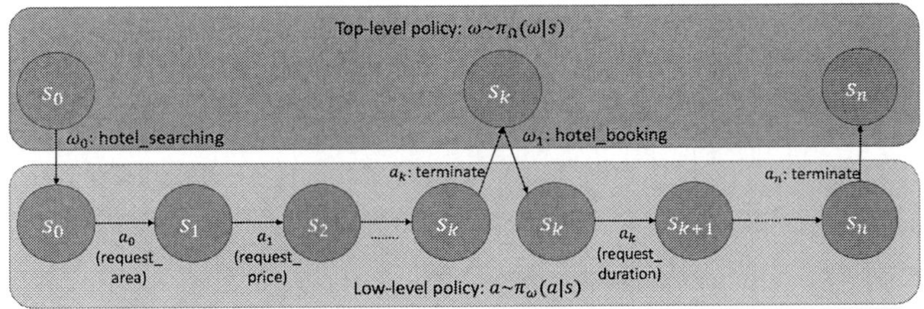

Figure 2: An example of the execution of our hierarchical dialogue policy in hotel reservation domain. At time $t = 0$ and $t = k$, given the belief state s_t, top-level policy π_Ω takes options ω_0 and ω_1, respectively. ω_0 lasts for k turns until its policy π_{ω_i} takes terminate action, while ω_1 lasts for $n - k$ turns.

further demonstrated that PVFs implicitly define options. PVF-based option discovery extracts options from the topology structure of the state space and is capable of providing dense *intrinsic* rewards for each option. The discovery process is given below.

Given a set of sampled state transitions, we construct an adjacency matrix W between belief states using Gaussian kernel. Then, we apply eigendecomposition to the combinatorial graph Laplacian of W. Each eigenvector (i.e. PVF) e_ω corresponds to an option with intrinsic reward function $r_i^\omega(s, s') = e_\omega[s'] - e_\omega[s]$ for a state transition from s to s'. Since our dialogue system has continuous belief states, we interpolate the value of eigenvectors to novel states using Nyström approximation (Mahadevan, 2007). The number of generated intrinsic reward functions is equal to the number of dialogue states in W, but we used intrinsic reward functions from eigenvectors with the smallest eigenvalues.

An option ω, which corresponds to an eigenvector e_ω, can be interpreted as a desire to reach a belief state s that has the highest value of $e_\omega[s]$ (Machado et al., 2017). In our experiment, such a state usually represents a dialogue goal or a state where user's inherent sub-domain changes (e.g. user starts the booking sub-domain once she finds the hotel satisfying her requirements).

3.3 Policy Learning with Intrinsic Rewards

To realize a dialogue framework that can discover effective and meaningful sub-domains, we feed PVFs into HRL-OC, then follows HRL-OC's learning procedure. Here, PVFs act as an internal evaluator of the dialogue policy. We formulate the $r(s, a)$ in Q_U to be $r(s, a) = \alpha r_i^\omega + (1 - \alpha)r_e$. Hereinafter, this model is denoted as

HRL-OC_PVF. We can regard HRL-OC as HRL-OC_PVF with $\alpha = 0$.

We also introduce alternative dialogue frameworks by applying the intrinsic rewards from PVFs directly to HRL algorithms. We train each policy π_ω in HRL using a specific intrinsic reward function r_i^ω. We implemented the hierarchical deep Q-networks (HRL-DQN; Kulkarni et al. (2016)), and policy gradient-DQN (HRL-PG_DQN), i.e., REINFORCE (Williams, 1992) as the top-level policy and DQN low-level policy. This assesses whether using only general-purpose intrinsic rewards, which are designed for exploration, is good for maximizing extrinsic rewards.

4 Experimental Setup

We conducted three evaluations on (i) the effectiveness of our autonomous sub-domain modeling compared to the manual sub-domain modeling, (ii) the performance difference between flat RL (i.e. without modeling) and the HRL with autonomous modeling, and (iii) the impact of using PVFs in discovering meaningful sub-domains.

4.1 Dialogue Domain

Following the setting in Budzianowski et al. (2017), we evaluated our proposed framework in the task of reserving a hotel room, which involves three sub-domains: searching for a hotel, booking, and payment. This domain has 13 constraint slots, that is 5 slots in hotel searching (price, kind, area, stars, hasparking), 5 slots in booking (day, hour, duration, peopleno, surname), and 3 slots in payment sub-domain (address, cardno, surname). Dialogue management over this dialogue domain is cast as a Markov Decision Process (MDP) with the following specification.

- *State*: the belief state $s \in \mathcal{S}$ with 239 dimensions that captures distribution over user's intents and requestable slots

- *Action set* $\mathcal{A}$: 44 dialogue actions, which consists of 8 slot-independent actions and 36 slot-dependent actions.

- *Reward*: -1 at each turn, and 0 or 20 (failed or success dialogue) at the end of dialogue

- *Discount factor* γ: 0.95

- *Maximum number of turns*: 30

4.2 User Simulator

We used an agenda-based user simulator (Schatzmann et al., 2007) with which the belief states perfectly capture the user intent. At the start of each dialogue, the simulated user randomly sets its goal that consists of searching for a hotel and either booking it or paying for it. User will proceed to the booking or payment sub-domain only after achieving the goal of the hotel searching sub-domain.

At the beginning of each sub-domain execution, the user's goal for that sub-domain is randomly generated using database. The agenda is populated by converting all goal constraints into *inform* acts, and all goal requests into *request* acts. For instance, *inform(price=moderate)* indicates a user requirement, and *request(address)* indicates the user asking for the address of the hotel returned by the system. Furthermore, in different dialogue episodes, the simulated user might convey its requirements (i.e. slot values) within a sub-domain to the dialogue system in different orders.

4.3 Dialogue Frameworks

Implementation As the benchmarks without sub-domain, we used flat RL algorithms (i.e. DQN, and PG with REINFORCE). For the benchmark with manual modeling, we used the framework introduced by Budzianowski et al. (2017), which utilized hierarchical Gaussian Process RL (HRL-GP).

All deep (flat and hierarchical) RL agents consist of 2 hidden layers (150 units in layer 1, and 75 (70 for PG) in layer 2). We used Adam optimizer, a mini-batch size of 32, and ϵ-greedy strategy for exploration. In HRL-DQN and HRL-PG_DQN agents, top-level and low-level policies have separate policy networks, each of which has 2 hidden layers as specified above. In these agents, the low-level policies share the same policy network. During execution, we pass the information of the option taken by the top-level policy to the low-level policy network. In HRL-OC and HRL-OC_PVF agents, the policy, the critic Q_Ω, and the termination networks share the same 2 hidden layers, but each of them has its own output layer.

For discovering PVFs, we generated state transition samples using hand-crafted rules (Ultes et al., 2017). We sub-sampled 1,000 unique states using trajectory sampling, and built W from them.

Prior Knowledge In the manual sub-domain modeling, the agent has two types of prior knowledge as follows.

- *sub-domains comprising a dialogue (i.e. hotels, booking, payment)*.

- *a valid action set for each sub-domain. All sub-domains share the same 8 slot-independent actions, but each of them has its own slot-dependent actions*.

To assess the impact of each type of prior knowledge, we implemented an HRL-GP framework that uses both types of knowledge and its variant HRL-GP2 that uses only sub-domain information. Both frameworks have separated policies to handle each sub-domain, but HRL-GP2 deals with a more complex situation since it has to select an action from the union of actions sets from all sub-domains, that is 44 dialogue actions in total. Unlike HRL-GP and HRL-GP2, our frameworks with autonomous modeling (HRL-DQN, HRL-PG_DQN, HRL-OC, HRL-OC_PVF) cannot access any prior knowledge. They initially perceive dialogues as a single domain problem and attempt to discover the meaningful sub-domains.

Evaluation We trained each policy in the frameworks for 30 iterations, each of which consists of 200 episodes. In the end of each iteration, we evaluated the performance of the models using 200 episodes. The metric we used for evaluation is the average success rate (SR) of dialogues.

Benchmark	SR(%)	Our framework	SR(%)
FlatRL (DQN)	66.9	HRL-DQN	49.6
FlatRL (PG)	62.0	HRL-PG_DQN	51.0
HRL-GP	84.8	HRL-OC	73.4
HRL-GP2	75.9	HRL-OC_PVF	72.1

Table 1: Highest SR of dialogue agents.

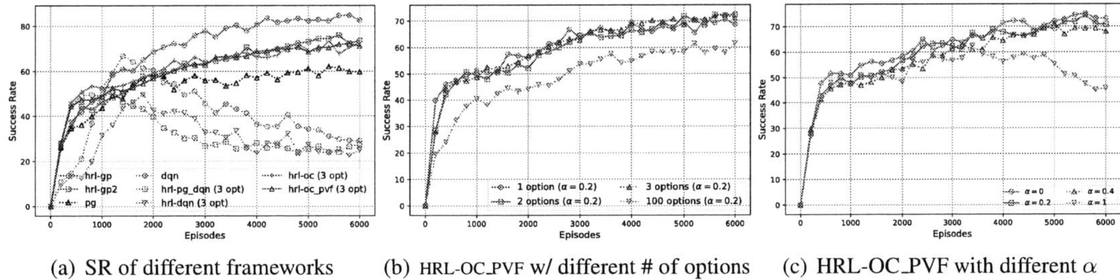

(a) SR of different frameworks   (b) HRL-OC_PVF w/ different # of options   (c) HRL-OC_PVF with different α

Figure 3: Learning curves of different dialogue frameworks

5 Experimental Results

5.1 Success Rate

The experimental results are shown in Table 1 and Figure 3. First, the flat RL, which is a DQN, achieved an SR of up to 66.9%, but it was unstable. The more stable flat framework, PG, obtained 62%. Our frameworks with autonomous modeling (HRL-OC and HRL-OC_PVF) outperformed flat RL significantly. However, HRL-DQN and HRL-PG_DQN performed worse than flat RL. This suggests that using only intrinsic rewards from PVFs is not adequate for constructing sub-domains that are effective in accumulating extrinsic rewards. Since HRL-OC optimizes its options for maximizing the accumulated extrinsic reward, it has a better SR compared to HRL-DQN and HRL-PG_DQN, which did not use any extrinsic rewards.

The frameworks with manual modeling, i.e. HRL-GP and HRL-GP2, reached an SR of 84.8 and 75.9%, respectively. One of the frameworks with autonomous modeling (i.e. HRL-OC) achieved up to 73.4%. Note that, in HRL-OC, all primitive actions are used for each option, which is the same as HRL-GP2. Although HRL-OC does not have any prior knowledge about sub-domains in a dialogue, it is competitive with the framework with strong supervision on sub-domains. This indicates that HRL-OC is able to learn effective sub-goals in a composite-task dialogue.

As shown in Figure 3, learning curves of different dialogue frameworks are examined. Figure 3(a) shows that HRL-OC and HRL-OC_PVF have steeper learning curves than HRL-GP in the first 1000 episodes, which indicates that our frameworks can shorten learning time. Figure 3(b) reports that the use of 2 or 3 options is optimal. Using too many options is harmful because the agent will require more episodes to learn the optimal policy over options. Figure 3(c) shows the effect of the interpolation ratio α for combining both *extrinsic* and *intrinsic* rewards on the SR. However, PVFs seem ineffective with respect to SR. To have $\alpha > 0$ reduces the SR of HRL-OC_PVF with 3 options.

5.2 Discovered Sub-domains

According to our observation, the HRL-OC_PVF with $\alpha = 0.2$, however, discovered more meaningful sub-domains than HRL-OC. To assess the meaningfulness of the discovered sub-domains, we examined how similar these sub-domains to those inherent in the user's agenda. We judge the similarity using the average dialogue turn distance between the turn when the user simulator enters a sub-domain and that when the agent switches sub-domains. The ideal case is to have a turn distance of 1, i.e., once a user enters a sub-domain, the agent responds by switching the active option in the next turn. Table 2 shows that compared to HRL-OC, the integration of PVFs results in sub-domains whose boundaries are similar to those of the user's sub-domains.

Table 3 shows that the integration of PVFs into HRL-OC makes the agent capable of changing the active sub-domain soon after the user enters a sub-domain. This indicates that PVFs can detect interesting belief states. In our further examination, PVFs successfully discover states that indicate dialogue goal, sub-task switching, and request of alternatives from the sampled transitions.

Agents	i^{th} iteration				
	1	2	3	4	5
HRL-OC	2.8	2.8	4.0	3.9	5.3
HRL-OC_PVF ($\alpha = 0.2$)	2.6	2.5	3.0	2.8	2.8
HRL-OC_PVF ($\alpha = 0.4$)	2.9	3.0	3.4	3.2	3.9

Table 2: Average turn distance between activation of user's sub-domains and agent's

13

User Goal			
slots	values	slots	values
hotel searching		payment	
price	don't care	address	bristol
kind	don't care	cardNo	600
area	west	surname	wilson
stars	3		
hasparking	don't care		
requestable slots			
name of the hotel			
hasinternet			
postcode			

S:	How may I help you?
U:	I'm looking for a hotel in west.
S:	A hotel in the west area right?
U:	Yes, and 3 stars.
S:	Would you like a hotel in the cheap, moderate, or expensive price range?
U:	any price
S:	Alpha-Milton guest house is a nice hotel.
U:	Does it have internet connection?
S:	It doesn't have internet.
U:	post code
S:	Their postcode is cb4 1xa.
U:	I'll pay with CC by Wilson. [user enters payment]
S:	How long is your stay?
U:	I don't care, my surname is Wilson.
S:	*Your name is Wilson right?* [system is in payment]
U:	*Yes, and my address is Bristol.*
	(...21 dialogue turns to CC alternatives...)
S:	*I will pay the room with CC 600 by Matt Wilson.*
U:	*Goodbye.*

Table 3: Sample dialogue by HRL-OC_PVF (S: agent, U: user). Different font styles and colors indicate different sub-domains activated by agent.

5.3 Discussion

Our experiments show that our proposed framework outperforms the baseline, and is competitive with with the framework with manually defined sub-domains. Even though the experiments are done using a simulator, the simulated user produces dialogue behavior realistic enough for training and testing. As mentioned in Section 4.2, the simulated user specifies its requirements within a sub-domain to the dialogue system in a random order. In addition, the simulator may also not specify several slot values. Such a behavior simulates a situation in which a human user forgets to specify some goal constraints.

In the experiments, the simulator has a constraint, that is it executes the inherent sub-domains in a fixed order. The fixed order of sub-domains, i.e. hotel search and then followed by either booking or payment, can still simulate the real world conversational data, since an activity of reserving a hotel room is commonly accomplished in such order. In other tasks, however, a fixed order of inherent sub-domains may not simulate the real conversation well. Nevertheless, even when the order of the inherent sub-domains are not fixed, we suggest that our proposed framework could still discover options that imitate the inherent sub-domains. This holds when the inherent sub-domains are executed sequentially, and the environment dynamics within each inherent sub-domain is invariant to the execution order of the sub-domains. Another challenging situation is when the inherent sub-domains are executed in an interleaved manner. This simulates a scenario in which a user frequently switches the active sub-domain before the current sub-domain is fulfilled. A further investigation is required to examine the options discovered in such a situation.

6 Conclusion

We proposed a framework that autonomously discovers sub-domains for a composite-task dialogue. Experimental results shows that our framework with autonomous modeling is competitive with the framework with manually defined sub-domains. Analysis also showed that the integration of PVFs leads to meaningful sub-domains.

For future work, we consider the adjustment of the PVFs construction, such as the distance metric between states, the construction of the adjacency matrix, and the use of successor representation (Dayan, 1993; Barreto et al., 2017). We may also need to further examine the discovered options when the inherent sub-domains are executed in several different manners and orders. Finally, it is also interesting to investigate the effectiveness of reusing the learned options in other related dialogue domains.

References

Pierre-Luc Bacon, Jean Harb, and Doina Precup. 2017. The Option-Critic Architecture. In *Proceedings of the 31st AAAI Conference on Artificial Intelligence*, pages 1726–1734, San Francisco, California, USA.

André Barreto, Will Dabney, Rémi Munos, Jonathan J. Hunt, Tom Schaul, David Silver, and Hado P. van Hasselt. 2017. Successor features for transfer in reinforcement learning. In *Advances in Neural Information Processing Systems 30*, pages 4058–4068, California, USA.

Paweł Budzianowski, Stefan Ultes, Pei-Hao Su, Nikola Mrkšić, Tsung-Hsien Wen, Iñigo Casanueva, Lina

Rojas-Barahona, and Milica Gašić. 2017. Subdomain Modelling for Dialogue Management with Hierarchical Reinforcement Learning. In *Proceedings of the 18th Annual SIGDIAL Meeting on Discourse and Dialogue*, pages 86–92, Saarbrücken, Germany.

Iñigo Casanueva, Paweł Budzianowski, Pei-Hao Su, Nikola Mrkšić, Tsung-Hsien Wen, Stefan Ultes, Lina Rojas-Barahona, Steve Young, and Milica Gašić. 2017. A Benchmarking Environment for Reinforcement Learning Based Task Oriented Dialogue Management. *CoRR*, abs/1711.1.

Heriberto Cuayáhuitl. 2009. *Hierarchical Reinforcement Learning for Spoken Dialogue Systems*. Ph.D. thesis, University of Edinburgh.

Heriberto Cuayáhuitl, Seunghak Yu, Ashley Williamson, and Jacob Carse. 2016. Deep Reinforcement Learning for Multi-Domain Dialogue Systems. In *Advances in Neural Information Processing Systems 29 Workshop on Deep Reinforcement Learning*, Barcelona, Spain.

Peter Dayan. 1993. Improving generalization for temporal difference learning: The successor representation. *Neural Computation*, 5(4):613–624.

Thomas G. Dietterich. 2000. Hierarchical Reinforcement Learning with the MAXQ Value Function Decomposition. *Journal of Artificial Intelligence Research*, 13:227–303.

M. Gasic, N. Mrksic, P. H. Su, D. Vandyke, T. H. Wen, and S. Young. 2016. Policy committee for adaptation in multi-domain spoken dialogue systems. *2015 IEEE Workshop on Automatic Speech Recognition and Understanding, ASRU 2015 - Proceedings*, pages 806–812.

Milica Gašić and Steve Young. 2014. Gaussian processes for POMDP-based dialogue manager optimization. *IEEE Transactions on Audio, Speech and Language Processing*, 22(1):28–40.

Tejas D. Kulkarni, Karthik R. Narasimhan, Ardavan Saeedi, and Joshua B. Tenenbaum. 2016. Hierarchical Deep Reinforcement Learning: Integrating Temporal Abstraction and Intrinsic Motivation. In *Advances in Neural Information Processing Systems 29*, pages 3675–3683, Barcelona, Spain.

Xiujun Li, Yun-Nung Chen, Lihong Li, Jianfeng Gao, and Asli Celikyilmaz. 2017. End-to-End Task-Completion Neural Dialogue Systems. In *Proceedings of the Eighth International Joint Conference on Natural Language Processing, IJCNLP*, pages 733–743, Taipei, Taiwan.

Marlos C. Machado, Marc G. Bellemare, and Michael Bowling. 2017. A Laplacian Framework for Option Discovery in Reinforcement Learning. In *Proceedings of the 34th International Conference on Machine Learning, ICML 2017*, pages 2295–2304, Sydney, NSW, Australia.

Sridhar Mahadevan. 2007. Proto-value Functions : A Laplacian Framework for Learning Representation and Control in Markov Decision Processes. *Journal of Machine Learning Research*, 8:2169–2231.

Volodymyr Mnih, Koray Kavukcuoglu, David Silver, Andrei A. Rusu, Joel Veness, Marc G. Bellemare, Alex Graves, Martin Riedmiller, Andreas K. Fidjeland, Georg Ostrovski, Stig Petersen, Charles Beattie, Amir Sadik, Ioannis Antonoglou, Helen King, Dharshan Kumaran, Daan Wierstra, Shane Legg, and Demis Hassabis. 2015. Human-level control through deep reinforcement learning. *Nature*, 518(7540):529–533.

Ronald Parr and Stuart Russell. 1997. Reinforcement learning with hierarchies of machines. In *Advances in Neural Information Processing Systems 10*, pages 1043–1049, Denver, Colorado, USA.

Baolin Peng, Xiujun Li, Lihong Li, Jianfeng Gao, Asli Celikyilmaz, Sungjin Lee, and Kam-Fai Wong. 2017. Composite Task-Completion Dialogue Policy Learning via Hierarchical Deep Reinforcement Learning. In *Proceedings of the 2017 Conference on Empirical Methods in Natural Language Processing, EMNLP 2017*, pages 2231–2240, Copenhagen, Denmark.

Jost Schatzmann, Blaise Thomson, Karl Weilhammer, Hui Ye, and Steve Young. 2007. Agenda-based user simulation for bootstrapping a pomdp dialogue system. In *Human Language Technologies 2007: The Conference of the North American Chapter of the Association for Computational Linguistics; Companion Volume, Short Papers*, pages 149–152. Association for Computational Linguistics.

Richard S. Sutton, Doina Precup, and Satinder Singh. 1999. Between MDPs and semi-MDPs: A framework for temporal abstraction in reinforcement learning. *Artificial Intelligence*, 112(1–2):181–211.

Stefan Ultes, Lina Rojas-barahona, Pei-Hao Su, David Vandyke, Dongho Kim, Paweł Budzianowski, and Nikola Mrksic. 2017. PyDial : A Multi-domain Statistical Dialogue System Toolkit. In *Proceedings of the 55th Annual Meeting of the Association for Computational Linguistics, ACL 2017*, pages 73–78, Vancouver, Canada.

Jason D. Williams, Kavosh Asadi, and Geoffrey Zweig. 2017. Hybrid Code Networks: practical and efficient end-to-end dialog control with supervised and reinforcement learning. In *Proceedings of the 55th Annual Meeting of the Association for Computational Linguistics, ACL 2017*, pages 665–677, Vancouver, Canada.

R. J. Williams. 1992. Simple statistical gradient-following algorithms for connectionist reinforcement learning. *Machine Learning*, 8:229–256.

Steve Young, Milica Gašić, Blaise Thomson, and Jason D. Williams. 2013. POMDP-based statistical

spoken dialog systems: A review. *Proceedings of
the IEEE*, 101(5):1160–1179.

Building Dialogue Structure from Discourse Tree of a Question

Boris Galitsky
Oracle Inc., Redwood Shores, CA USA

Boris.galitsky@oracle.com

Dmitry Ilvovsky
National Research University Higher School
of Economics, Moscow, Russia
dilvosky@hse.ru

Abstract

In this section we propose a reasoning-based approach to a dialogue management for a customer support chat bot. To build a dialogue scenario, we analyze the discourse tree (DT) of an initial query of a customer support dialogue that is frequently complex and multi-sentence. We then enforce rhetorical agreement between DT of the initial query and that of the answers, requests and responses. The chat bot finds answers, which are not only relevant by topic but also suitable for a given step of a conversation and match the question by style, communication means, experience level and other domain-independent attributes. We evaluate a performance of proposed algorithm in car repair domain and observe a 5 to 10% improvement for single and three-step dialogues respectively, in comparison with baseline approaches to dialogue management.

1 Introduction

Answering questions, a chat bot needs to reason to properly select answers from candidates. In industrial applications of search, reasoning is often substituted by learning from conversational logs or user choices. It helps to make search more relevant as long as a similar question has been asked many times. If there is no data on previous similar question, which is frequently the case, a chat bot needs to apply some form of reasoning to select from candidate answers (Wilks, 1999).

Most frequent type of reasoning is associated with topical relevance. It requires ontology and is domain-specific. Difficulties in building domain ontologies are well known, and in this paper we take a different reasoning-based approach. Once a set of candidate answers or replies is available, how to select most suitable ones? The suitability criteria are two-dimensional: 1) topical relevance; and 2) an appropriateness not associated with top-

ic but instead connected with communicative discourse. Whereas topical relevance has been thoroughly investigated, chat bot's capability to maintain the cohesive flow, style and merits of conversation is an underexplored area.

When a question (Q) is detailed and includes multiple sentences, there are certain expectations concerning the style of an answer (A). Although topical agreement between questions and answers has been extensively addressed, a correspondence in style and suitability for the given step of a dialogue between questions and answers has not been thoroughly explored. In this study we focus on assessment of the cohesiveness of the Q/A flow, which is important for a chat bots supporting longer conversation. When an answer is in a style disagreement with a question, a user can find this answer inappropriate even when a topical relevance is high. Matching rhetorical structures of questions and answers is a systematic way to implement high-level reasoning for dialogue management, to be explored in this work.

A problem in communicative discourse occurs mostly for complex questions (Chali et al., 2009; Galitsky, 2017), arising in miscommunication, a lack of understanding, and requiring clarification, argumentation and other means to bring the answer's author point across. Rhetorical disagreement is associated with a broken dialogue and is usually evident via the means an answer is communicated, explained or backed up.

Our paper is organized as follows. In Section 2 we discuss basic notions of discourse tree text representation. In Section 3 we consider details our approach to building a dialogue based on discourse trees. In Section 4 we present evaluation results for the one of the Q/A tasks.
The system described in this paper is available on our GitHub[1].

---

[1] https://github.com/bgalitsky/relevance-based-on-parse-trees

Proceedings of the 2018 EMNLP Workshop SCAI: The 2nd Int'l Workshop on Search-Oriented Conversational AI, pages 17–23
Brussels, Belgium, October 31, 2018. ©2018 Association for Computational Linguistics

2 Discourse Tree and Rhetorical Structure

To represent the linguistic features of a text, we used *Rhetorical relations* (RR) between the parts of the sentences, obtained as a *discourse tree*. We relied on Rhetorical Structure Theory (RST, Mann and Thompson, 1988) and deployed state-of-the-art rhetorical parsers (Joty et al., 2013; Surdeanu et al., 2015) to build these discourse trees automatically.

Rhetorical Structure Theory models the logical organization of text, a structure employed by a writer relying on relations between parts of text. RST simulates text coherence by forming a hierarchical connected structure of texts via discourse trees. Rhetorical relations are split into coordinate and subordinate classes; these relations hold across two or more text spans and therefore implement coherence. These text spans are called *elementary discourse units* (EDUs).

Clauses in a sentence and sentences in a text are logically connected by the author. The meaning of a given sentence is related to that of the previous and following sentences. This logical relation between clauses is called the coherence structure of the text. RST is one of the most popular theories of discourse and is based on tree-like discourse structures called discourse trees. The leaves of a DT correspond to EDUs, the contiguous atomic text spans. Adjacent EDUs are connected by coherence rhetorical relations (e.g., *Attribution, Sequence*), forming higher-level discourse units. These units are then also subject to this relation-linking. EDUs linked by a relation are then differentiated based on their relative importance: *nuclei* represent the core parts of the relation, whereas *satellites* represent the peripheral ones.

Let's consider small example of a discourse tree for the text. For the question
"What does Clinton foundation really do" one can find the following answer:
Becoming a Secretary of State, Hillary Clinton promised to distance herself from the Clinton Foundation. However, Clinton continued to have a cozy relationship with the foundation, having the US foreign policy for sale there. According to some sources, Clinton was granting access and favors to major Clinton Foundation donors.

The discourse tree of an answer is presented on Figure 1 is based on *Elaboration* and *Background* rhetorical relations.

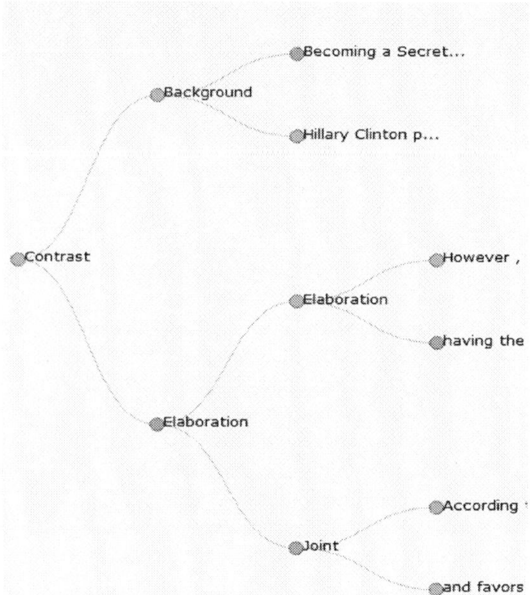

Figure 1: Example of a discourse tree

3 Building Dialogue Structure with Discourse

3.1 Maintaining Discourse in a Dialogue

Once we have a detailed initial question, we frequently can determine which direction we can take a given dialogue. If an answer is formulated in a straight-forward way, then a definitional or factual answer is to follow.

Otherwise, if a question includes a doubt, a request to dig deeper into a topic, or to address a controversy, the dialogue should be handled with replies including attribution, communicating a contrast, explicit handling of what was expected and what actually happened. Hence from Rhetorical relations in initial query the chat bot can select one set of answers over the other not only to cover the main topic, but to also address associated issues raised by the user. It can be done even if the initial query is short and its DT is trivial.

Now imagine for each of answers we obtain multiple candidates, with distinct entities. How the chat bot would know which entity in an answer would be of a higher interest to a user? The chat bot need to include a clarification procedure.

For a single Q/A pair, one can refer to their coordination as rhetorical agreement (Galitsky,

2017). For the dialogue management problem, where a sequence of answers A_i need to be in agreement with an initial question Q, we refer the proposed solution as *maintaining communicative discourse in a dialogue*. It includes three components:

1) Finding a sequence of answers A_i to be in agreement with an initial question Q

2) Maintaining clarification procedure where for each i we have multiple candidate answers and need to rely on a user to select which one to deliver.

3) Allowing the chat bot user to specify additional constraints, formulate more specific questions as answers A_i are being delivered.

3.2 Building Dialogue Structure in Customer Support Dialogues

Let us start with an example of a *customer support dialogue*, where a customer support agent tries to figure out a root cause of a problem (Fig.2.). Customer support scenarios form a special class of dialogues where customers attempt to resolve certain problems, get their questions answered and get to their desired outcomes unreachable using default business procedures. Customer support dialogues frequently start with initial question, a multi-sentence statement of problems Q, from which experienced customer support personal frequently plan a resolution strategy.

The personnel come up with a sequence of recommendations and explanations for them addressing customer concerns expressed in Q. Also, the personnel comes up with some questions to the customer to adjust their recommendations to the needs expressed by the customer in Q. Frequently, due to diverse nature of most businesses, it is hard to find a dialogue in a customer support problem which addresses this exact problem. Therefore, individual answers and recommendations from the previous customer support sessions are used, not the whole such sessions, in the majority of cases. Hence the customer support dialogue management cannot be reduced to the problem of finding sufficiently similar dialogue and just following it: instead, actual construction of a dialogue to address Q is required most of times.

The system finds candidate answers with the keywords and phrases from the initial query, such as *Google Earth, cannot see, attention* and others. Which candidate answers would be the best to match the communicative discourse of the query?

A customer support dialogue can be represented as a sequence:

$$Q, A_1, C_1, A_2, C_2, ...,$$

where Q is an initial query describing a problem, A_1 is an initial recommendation and also a clarification request, C_1 is a response to this request, A_2 is a consecutive recommendation and clarification request, C_2 is a response to A_2 and possibly a further question, and so forth. Our goal is to simulate a broad spectrum of dialogue structures via correspondence of discourse trees of utterances. This way once Q is given, the chat bot can maintain the sequence of answers A_i for Q.

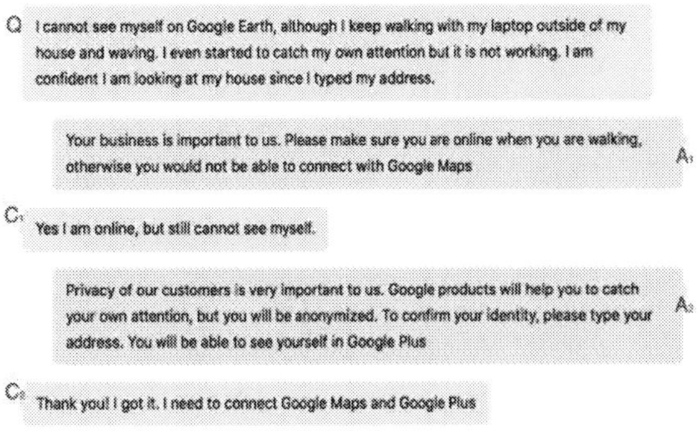

Figure 2: An example of a customer support dialogue

3.3 Finding a Sequence of Answers to be in Agreement with Question

DT for the Q, and DT for the sequence of two answers A_1 and A_2 from our example are shown in Fig. 3. Arrows show which chains of DT-Q determine which chains of DT-A_i.

We will now demonstrate that a *chain* of nodes in DT-Q is determining a corresponding chain of nodes in DT-A. This chain is defined as a path in a DT. The chain of RRs with entities are *Elaboration [see myself Google Earth]-Contrast [walk laptop house]-Temporal [waiving]* on the top of DT-Q is addressed by the chain *Elaboration [online]-Same_Unit [walking]-Contract [Otherwise, not able connect]* in the first answer A_1. We use the label *RR [abbreviated phrase]* for each node of a chain in DT. Notice that not only *RRs* are supposed to be coordinated but the entities in *phrases* as well.

The second answer A_2 attempts to address in a complete way the issues raised in the second part of Q. The first mapping is between the chain RR *Elaboration [catch my attention] -Contrast [not working]* in Q and the chain *Elaboration [catch my attention] - Contrast [anonymized]*.

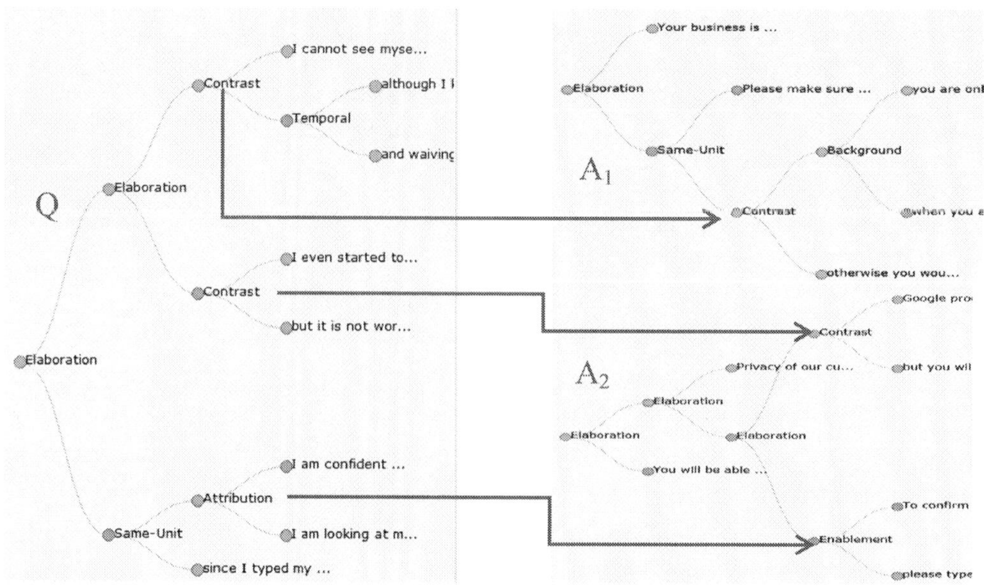

Figure 3: Discourse tree of a question Q (on the left) and a sequence (pair) of combined discourse trees (on the right) for the answers A_i.

The main observation here is that the question itself gives us a hint on a possible sequence of answers, or on the order the issues in the question are raised. One can look at the *DT-Q* and form a dialogue scenario (*first do this, obtain confirmation, then do that …*). Since a dialogue is built from available answer fragments (e.g. from conversational logs), we take candidate answers, form candidate DTs from them and see if they match DT-Q. Hence a single nontrivial DT-Q determines *both DT-A₁ and DT-A₂*. We refer to this capability as *determining the structure of a dialogue* (the structure of a sequence of answers) by the initial Q. We intentionally selected this anecdotal, meaningless example of a customer support dialogue to demonstrate that a full "understanding" of a query is not required; instead, the logical structure of inter-relations between the entities in this query is essential to find a sequence of answers.

Is it possible to come up with a rule for DT-A$_i$ given DT-Q, to formalize the notion of "addressing" an issue in Q by an A? A simple rule would be for a chain of rhetorical relations for an A to be a sub-chain of that of a Q, also maintaining respective entities. But this rule turns out to be too restrictive and even invalid in some cases. Our observation is that *DT–A* does not have to copy *DT-Q* or its parts, but instead have some comple-

mentarity features. There are two types of considerations for *DT-A$_i$* :

1) Each nontrivial RR in Q needs to be addressed by a RR in *DT-A$_i$.*

2) There should be a rhetorical agreement between Q and A_i, defined for a search engine.

Whereas rhetorical agreement introduces a pair-wise constraint that can be learned from examples of good and bad *Q/A* pairs (Galitsky, 2017), we extend it to one-to-many relation between a single Q and a sequence of A_i.

For an RR in *DT-A$_i$* to address an RR in Q, it does not necessarily need to be the same RR but it should not be a default RR such as *Elaboration* or *Joint. Attribution* and *Enablement*, for example, can address *Contrast*.

Also, for a *RR(EDU$_{q1}$, EDU$_{q2}$)* in Q to be covered by *RR(EDU$_{ai1}$, EDU$_{ai2}$)* in A_i, entities E should be shared between *EDU$_{q1}$* and *EDU$_{ai1}$* : $EDU_{q1} \cap EDU_{ai1} = E : E \neq \varnothing.$

3.4   Searching for the Answers for Dialogue construction

Once we established the rules for addressing RRs in Q, we can implement search for a series of answers A_i given Q. Assuming we have a corpus of dialogues with utterances tagged as A or Q, it should be indexed offline in at least two following fields: 1) keywords of A and 2) RRs with their EDUs.

Then once we receive Q, build DT-Q, and split DT-Q into subtrees each of which contains at least single non-default RR. Then for each *subtree-DT-Q* we form a query against these fields:

1) Keywords from the *EDU-subtree-DT-Q;*

2) Non-default RR from *subtree-DT-Q.*

For each candidate answer satisfying the query we still have to verify

rhetorical_agreement(subtree-DT-Q, A_i).

Once the answer A_i is selected and given to the user, user responds with C_i which in general case contains some clarification expressed in A_i and also an additional question part Q_i . The latter would then require an additional answer which should be added to A_i if it has been already computed.

The high-level view of the ***search algorithm*** that supports the dialogue is as follows:

1) Build DT-Q;
2) Split DT-Q into parts Q_1, Q_2,... to correspond to A_1, A_2,...;
3) Form search query for A_1 from Q_1 in the form *RST-relation [phrase]* ;
4) Run the search against the set of dialogue utterances and obtain the list of candidate answers for the first step $A_{1\text{candidate}}$;
5) Build DT-$A_{1\text{candidate}}$ for each candidate and approve/reject each based on *rhetorical_agreement (DT–Q, DT-$A_{1\text{candidate}}$)*. Select the best candidate A_1;
6) Respond to the user with the selected A_1 and receive C_1;
7) Form search query for A_2 from Q_1&C_1;
8) Repeat steps 4) and 5) for A_2 , respond to the user with the selected A_2 and receive C_2;
9) Conclude the session or switch to a human agent

Hence the dialogue management problem can be formulated as a search with constraints on DTs and can be implemented via traditional search engineering means plus discourse parsing, when an adequate set of chat logs is available. Discourse-tree based dialogue management does not cover all possibilities of assuring smooth dialogue flows but provides a plausible mechanism to select suitable utterances from the available set. It allows avoiding solving NL generation problem for dialogues that is a source of a substantial distortion of conversation flow and a noise in meaning of utterances.

In this paper we suggested a mechanism to build a dialogue structure where the first utterance formulated a detailed Q requiring some

knowledge and explanation. If this Q is detailed enough the chat bot can attempt to find a sequence of answers to address all issues raised in Q.

3.5 Clarification-driven Dialogue

Some goals related to dialogue management do not need to be achieved via DTs. For example, an implementation of *clarification* feature can be hard-coded and does not require specific RRs. When a user asks a broad question, the chat bot forms topics for this user to choose from. Once such a topic is selected, the full answer is provided.

We have built an algorithm for mapping $Q \rightarrow A_i$. When multiple valid candidate answers for each i obtained, a clarification procedure is needed to have the user selected A_{ij} from the set A_i of answers or recommendations valid from both relevance and rhetorical agreement perspectives. We now update step 6) of the search algorithm which requests clarification when multiple suitable answers are available:

6) Respond to the user with the list of choices selected $\{A_{1s}|s=0..n\}$ and receive clarification result with possibly additional constraint request C_1 (which includes the choice A_{1j})

4 Evaluation of Dialogue Construction

4.1 Example from Car Repair Domain

As we proceed to evaluation, we will share an example of a dialogue from the evaluation domain of recommendations on car repair. Key characteristics of this domain are an importance of accurate recommendation, adequate dialogue structure, lesser bios than in other domains such as political, and an availability of a complete and accurate coverage of a broad spectrum of car problems. We provide an example of a sample dialogue:

Q_1: *I have checked the spark plugs, replaced the battery, also replaced ignition coils and the solenoid, but I still could not start my car.*
A_1: *Is the engine getting spark and fuel? Will it start for a couple seconds using starting fluid?*
Q_2: *It did at first but not anymore. What should I do?*
A_2 : *Check fuel pressure. But if no pressure, check the fuel pump for possible fault. If you have fuel pressure, then using a node light make sure you have injector pulse. The light should blink when cranking. If light is not blinking does the check engine light come on with key on and engine off? If no light then look for a bad main relay or no power - to the engine control module.*

In this example, since Q_1 includes rhetorical relation of *Contrast* (something is done correctly but still not working), detailed answer should include *Contrast, Condition,* or other RR that would address *Contrast* in Q. A certain recommended action is performed either correctly or incorrectly and both these cases need to be addressed.

4.2 Dataset and Results

We formed a dataset of 9300 Q/A pairs related to car repair recommendations from www.2carpros.com. These pairs were extracted from dialogues as first and second utterance, so that the question is $7 - 15$ keywords and answer is 3 to 6 sentences. This resource was obtained to train a dialogue support system but it also proved to be useful to evaluate search. The dataset is available online [2] in our GitHub.

To automate the relevance assessment, we considered the dialogue built *correctly* if an *actual* dialogue from the dataset is formed, given the first Q as a seed. Otherwise, if the sequence of utterances does not occur in the dataset, we consider it to be *incorrect*. There are some deficiencies of this approach since some actual dialogs are illogical and some synthetic dialogues built from distinct ones can be plausible, but it allows avoiding a manual tagging and construction of dialogues. The number of formed answers is limit to three: once initial Q is given, the system forms A_1, a set of A_{2i} and A_{3j}. A_1 is followed by the actual C_1 from the dialogue Q, so the proper A_2 needs to be selected. Analogously, once actual C_2 (if applicable) is provided, proper A_3 needs to be selected.

As a first baseline approach, we selected dialogue construction based on keyword similarity only, without taking into account a dialogue flow by considering a DT-Q. As a second baseline approach, we augment keyword similarity with linguistic relevance by computing maximal common sub-parse trees between the Q and A_i (Galitsky, 2013; Galitsky et al., 2013).

For the selected dataset, baseline approach is capable of building correct scenarios in the cases when similar keywords or similar linguistic phrases deliver the only dialogue scenario that is correct. On the contrary, *DT-Q* dialogue formation does not always succeed because some scenarios deviate from actual ones in the training set, alt-

---

[2] https://github.com/bgalitsky/relevance-based-on-parse-trees/blob/master/examples/CarRepairData_AnswerAnatomyDataset2.csv.zip

hough they are still plausible. Hence we see 10 and 5% improvement over the first and second baselines respectively for a basic, single-step scenario (Table 1).

Dialog type	Q-A	Q-A$_1$-C$_1$	Q-A$_1$-C$_1$-A$_2$	Q-A$_1$-C$_1$-A$_2$-C$_2$-A$_3$
Baseline 1	62.3±4.5	60.2±5.6	58.2±5.0	52.5±5.7
Baseline 2	67.0+4.8	63.8±4.8	57.3±5.3	55.6±5.9
DT-Q dialog formation	72.3±5.6	70.3±4.9	65.1±5.5	65.9±5.7

Table 1: Correctness of dialogue construction

As scenario becomes more complex, the chance that the proper scenario is selected by topic relevance decreases. At the same time, overall scenario formation complexity increases, and therefore an error rate for *DT-Q* approach increases as well. For the most complex, 3-step dialogue scenarios, *DT-Q* approach exceeds the baselines by 13 and 10% respectively.

5 Conclusions

In this paper we discovered that a dialogue structure could be built from the discourse tree of an initial question. This structure is built on top of the default conversational structure implementing such features as clarification, personalization or recommendation. For personalization, for a user query, the customer support chat bot system reduces the list of resolution scenarios based on what information is available for the given user. Chat bot recommendation scenario proposes a solution to a problem by finding the one accepted by users similar to the current one. Clarification, personalization and recommendation scenario covers only a small portion of plausible customer support scenarios. Discourse analysis of dialogues support dialogue scenario management in a universal way, for a broad range of available text fragments and previously accumulated responses.

Acknowledgments

The work of Dmitry Ilvovsky was supported by RFBR grants 16-29-12982 and 16-01-00583 and was prepared within the framework of the Basic Research Program at the National Research University Higher School of Economics (HSE) and supported within the framework of a subsidy by the Russian Academic Excellence Project '5-100'.

References

Wilks, Y. A. (Ed.). 1999. *Machine conversations.* Kluwer.

Mann, William and Sandra Thompson. 1988. *Rhetorical structure theory: Towards a functional theory of text organization. Text* - Interdisciplinary Journal for the Study of Discourse, 8(3):243–281.

Joty, Shafiq R, Giuseppe Carenini, Raymond T Ng, and Yashar Mehdad. 2013. *Combining intra-and multi- sentential rhetorical parsing for document-level discourse analysis.* In ACL (1), pages 486–496.

Mihai Surdeanu, Thomas Hicks, and Marco A. Valenzuela-Escarcega. 2015 *Two Practical Rhetorical Structure Theory Parsers.* NAACL HLT.

Chali, Y. Shafiq R. Joty, and Sadid A. Hasan. 2009. *Complex question answering: unsupervised learning approaches and experiments.* J. Artif. Int. Res. 35, 1 (May 2009), 1-47.

Boris Galitsky. 2017. *Discovering Rhetorical Agreement between a Request and Response.* Dialogue & Discourse 8(2) 167-205.

B Galitsky, D Ilvovsky, SO Kuznetsov, F Strok. 2013. *Matching sets of parse trees for answering multi-sentence questions.* RANLP-2013.

Boris Galitsky. 2013. *Machine Learning of Syntactic Parse Trees for Search and Classification of Text.* Engineering Application of Artificial Intelligence.

A Methodology for Evaluating Interaction Strategies of Task-Oriented Conversational Agents

Marco Guerin[1,2], Sara Falcone[1], Bernardo Magnini[1]
[1]Fondazione Bruno Kessler, Via Sommarive 18, Povo, Trento — Italy
[2]AdeptMind Scholar, Canada
{guerini,sfalcone,magnini}@fbk.eu

Abstract

In task-oriented conversational agents, more attention has been usually devoted to assessing task effectiveness, rather than to *how* the task is achieved. However, conversational agents are moving towards more complex and human-like interaction capabilities (e.g. the ability to use a formal/informal register, to show an empathetic behavior), for which standard evaluation methodologies may not suffice. In this paper, we provide a novel methodology to assess - in a completely controlled way - the impact on the quality of experience of agent's interaction strategies. The methodology is based on a within subject design, where two slightly different transcripts of the same interaction with a conversational agent are presented to the user. Through a series of pilot experiments we prove that this methodology allows fast and cheap experimentation/evaluation, focusing on aspects that are overlooked by current methods.

1 Introduction

The evaluation of task-oriented conversational agents is usually focused on measuring their effectiveness, either at the single turn level - see for example (Wen et al., 2015; Frampton and Lemon, 2006; Chen et al., 2013) - or at the level of the whole interaction - e.g success rate (Dybkjaer et al., 2004). Still, as conversational agents are becoming more complex and human-like (Bowden et al., 2017; Romero et al., 2017; Cercas Curry et al., 2017), these evaluation methodologies may not suffice. In this paper, we present a framework for evaluating interaction strategies of conversational agents during their development phase. Our approach combines in a novel way methodologies already tested and validated, and is based on

Proceedings of the 2018 EMNLP Workshop SCAI: The 2nd International Workshop on Search-Oriented Conversational AI, 978-1-948087-75-9

a pairwise comparison of manually curated transcripts of possible interactions.

On the one hand, our methodology is inspired by the Human-Computer-Interaction (HCI) literature by dividing the evaluation of a system in the *Quality of Service* (QoS) and *Quality of Experience* (QoE) dimensions (Moller et al., 2009). The former corresponds to the efficiency of the system, while the latter refers to the way in which the system accomplishes the task. In dialogue systems evaluation the traditional focus is on the QoS, while in this work we deal also with the QoE. On the other hand, we take advantage of crowdsourcing methodologies, a fast and cheap way we use to evaluate interactions while maintaining complete control over experimental conditions – by using a design similar to A/B testing, but in a 'within subject' condition. In this setting two slightly different versions of the same interaction with a conversational agent are presented to the user for a pairwise comparison (e.g. the same interaction using a formal/informal register). Unlike standard Wizard of Oz (WoZ) or lab experiments, the user does not directly interact with the system, rather s/he reads the manually curated transcript, so to eliminate confounding variables and make data collection much faster.

The paper is structured as follows: in Section 2 we discuss some of the main approaches used in the evaluation of conversational agents. In Section 3 and 4 we present our framework and provide some pilot experiments respectively. Finally in Section 5 we discuss the advantages of the approach in light of the results of the experiments.

2 Related Works

Several frameworks to evaluate dialogue systems have been proposed. So far, evaluation mainly focused on implemented components/systems and

Proceedings of the 2018 EMNLP Workshop SCAI: The 2nd Int'l Workshop on Search-Oriented Conversational AI, pages 24–32
Brussels, Belgium, October 31, 2018. ©2018 Association for Computational Linguistics

followed different criteria taken from other research fields, such as machine translation (Wen et al., 2016), human-computer interaction (Allen et al., 2001), user experience and interfaces design (Skantze, 2005). The fact that these methodologies are not designed to evaluate dialogue system, can affect the results - for example, machine translation metrics do not correlate well with human judgments (Liu et al., 2016). Another common aspect of these approaches is that they rely on a complete implementation of the system to evaluate aspects such as efficiency (Raux et al., 2006), quality (Shawar and Atwell, 2007) or both (Silvervarg and Jönsson, 2011), while in the case of our interaction strategies it would be useful to have a simulation approach that allows to predict the possible impact of such strategies. In the following we first discuss standard methodologies for implemented systems, then methodologies using simulation, and finally evaluation in related fields that inspired our approach.

Evaluation of implemented systems. Among the metrics used for evaluating specific components of a system we can briefly mention: (i) *fluency/grammaticality* of the generated sentences in the NLG step of the interaction, that can be done either manually (Wen et al., 2015) or in a semiautomatic way, as in (Riezler et al., 2003); (ii) *slots correctly realized*, an automatic evaluation of the NLG component (Scheffler and Young, 2002; Frampton and Lemon, 2006); (iii) *slots correctly recognized*, an automatic technique used to evaluate the NLU component (Levin and Pieraccini, 1997; Chen et al., 2013).

Among the metrics used for evaluating whole interactions there is *success rate*. It can be based on objective automatic measures or on a subjective evaluation made by users evaluating the system according to guidelines provided by the experimenter (Dybkjaer et al., 2004).

Finally, a framework worth mentioning is PARADISE (Walker et al., 1997) that is specifically devoted to spoken dialogue systems (while in our work we consider text based interactions only). This work focuses on metrics such as task success rate and dialogue cost (e.g. dialogue time, number of utterances, agent response delay) to evaluate the quality of a system. With regard to spoken dialogue systems, the use of crowdsourcing for collecting preference judgments has already been explored, for example in (Trippas et al., 2017; Chuklin et al., 2018; Alfonseca, 2017)

Evaluation through simulation. If the system is still at an early stage of development, a viable solution is to use *WoZ experiments* (Dahlbäck et al., 1993; Paek, 2001; Raux et al., 2006), in which the interaction is simulated and users are prepared on how to behave. Still, this approach suffers of some main drawbacks: (i) the need for conducting several time-consuming interactions to get stable results; (ii) the possible measured improvements of the system can still be biased by confounding variables; (iii) it is difficult for wizards to provide consistent responses across sessions; (iv) 'behavior instructions' should be prepared and given to the wizard and possibly to each single user[1] (v) these 'behavior instructions' cannot describe every single reaction, but must try to control typical situations.

Evaluation in related fields. Our design leverages in a novel way elements used in several fields.

Two variants testing with controlled stimulus material. In the MT field, the work by (Graham et al., 2013) used a 'within subject' design where each evaluator was sometimes presented with a small random textual variation (control condition) of a translation they were already exposed to (experimental condition). This methodology was used to evaluate the quality of raters' judgments. Closely to our approach, the MT evaluation campaign presented in (Bojar et al., 2016) used expert annotators for *pairwise* system comparisons denoting whether a system A was judged better than, worse than, or equivalent to another system B. In this case the two conditions were presented simultaneously, side by side, rather than in a random sequential order as in (Graham et al., 2013). Other seminal approaches - using direct comparison of stimulus materials via pairwise comparison - is presented in the realm of affective NLG (Van Der Sluis and Mellish, 2010), and in the domain of persuasive NLP (Tan et al., 2014). Still, both works used this procedure just for the validation of stimulus material and made resort to traditional evaluation procedures for the final evaluation. Finally, in the realm of persuasive NLG a crowdsourced approach based on A/B testing

---

[1] e.g. 'pretend you are sad because ...' so to trigger the desired system response, such as empathy. In fact, if the user were totally 'free' to interact with the Wizard s/he could miss the functionality under inspection – Still, guiding the user during the interaction strongly affects its naturalness. On the other hand Wizards require significant training so to respond in a way that is credible and consistent.

and focused on ecological validity is presented in (Guerini et al., 2012). This approach, however, uses a between-subject design, where subjects are presented with just one stimulus material.

Transcripts and 'third party' evaluation. Two approaches that use transcripts of the conversation, instead of a direct interaction with the agent, are presented in (Jurčíček et al., 2011; Yang et al., 2010). These works compared lab experiments with crowdsourced ones - in the scenario of spoken dialogue systems - showing that the results in the former (direct interaction with the system) are comparable with the results in the latter (third party users reading transcriptions). Similarly, in (Pragst et al., 2017), the authors focus on a WoZ evaluation of the interaction strategies of an embodied conversational agents. Users were presented with the video of an embodied conversational agent interacting with a human user (the agent was guided by a Wizard and the user was an instructed actor). The subjects have to evaluate the interactions answering to a survey using a Likert scale. In this experiment, as in the previous one, the subject is third-party evaluator who did not directly entered the interaction.

3 Proposed Solution

Starting from the advantages and limitations of the previous approaches, we designed a new framework to evaluate a task-oriented dialogue system from the point of view of the strategies of interaction. In our framework the dependent variables are QoS and QoE aspects instantiated in a questionnaire to be evaluated by the subjects, while the independent variables are the interaction strategies that are instantiated in the stimulus material.

In particular, we propose a methodology in which the transcripts of two versions of the interaction with a conversational agent (e.g. one using a formal language and one using an informal one, one being empathetic and one not) are presented to the user, to see if one version is preferred over the other. The core idea of the approach is that, differently from WoZ studies, the subjects must *read* the transcripts of the interaction rather than directly *interacting* with the agent. This is required in order to grant complete control over the experiment (transcripts can be manually curated so to meet stringent control criteria). The two versions must maintain all aspects and wording of the interaction the same (apart from those affected by the modal-

ity being tested), including the outcome (e.g. success of the interaction) so that, if one version is preferred over the other, we can conclude that the effect of preference is solely due to the variable of interest (e.g. the "formality level" of the language, the empathy of the agent) and not to other factors.

The procedure for setting up an experiment is:

1. *Control conditions.* Create one or more control conditions for each interaction strategy to be tested: either a transcript of a real interaction with an existing system or a possible interaction with the planned one.
2. *Experimental conditions.* Create an experimental condition that is the manually curated counterpart of the control condition. As stated, changes in the wording should be minimal and must always reflect the interaction strategy to be tested. Changes can be of two types: (a) *substitution* of portions of system's utterances with new coherent portions that represent the experimental condition (e.g. change an informal greeting with a formal one) or (b) *insertion* of new portions of text in system's utterances.
3. *Questionnaire.* Prepare a questionnaire that includes questions about the Qos and QoE dimensions of interest.
4. *Crowdsource.* Built a task on a crowdsourcing platform with a pairwise comparison design and the questionnaire subministered after each comparison.

Many interaction strategies can be analysed to test our approach. We decided to focus on five of them, those we deemed most interesting and impactful on the pragmatics of the dialogue and for which an effect should be detected (Radziwill and Benton, 2017), so to test if our methodology is able to capture such effect.

4 Experiments

In this section we describe a showcase experiment for our methodology, where we evaluated 5 possible variants of CH1, a conversational agent that we implemented in order to calculate the carbohydrates of user's meals. We set up a two variants testing for each independent variable, where we provided to the subjects of the experiment the transcripts of some conversations between a human user and CH1. Before starting the experiment, the user received a short text describing the task.

4.1 Interaction Strategies

Five strategies, together with their linguistic parameters, were analyzed. The transcripts of the experimental condition were realized by two expert linguists, following the substitution/insertion instructions described in Section 3.

Empathy can be defined as the ability of a conversational agent to adapt to the user feelings and also to provide flexible emotionally-coloured responses for different purposes (Callejas et al., 2011). There exist many different ways in which emotions are defined, represented and managed within dialogue systems (Meira and Canuto, 2015; Barrett et al., 2007). Usually, the recognition is based on the manifestation of the user emotion, which can be processed considering linguistic (Balahur et al., 2014) and paralinguistic cues (Schuller et al., 2013).

Formality in linguistics is expressed through the choice of lexical expressions. According to the context, the speaker can use a specific linguistic register, style and lexicon (Heylighen and Dewaele, 1999). In order to detect the formality of a text there exist different strategies. One is to detect the average of deixis for each grammatical category of words (Heylighen and Dewaele, 1999); another is to use words length and latinate affix (Brooke et al., 2010).

Facing is the ability to tackle situations in which the conversational agent has not a proper or preset answer (Morrissey and Kirakowski, 2013). We can observe two kinds of facing for unexpected users' input: (i) the agent is not able to recognize the intention and makes resort to a default answer, e.g. "Sorry I do not understand, could you repeat?"; (ii) the agent is able to recognize the intention and it provides a suitable/contextual answer even if it is not endowed with the skills to solve it.

Vocabulary Extension concerns agent's ability to learn new words during the conversation and use them appropriately in the ongoing (Riccardi and Hakkani-Tur, 2005). For example, CH1 needs to know a huge variety of food names (from specific names such as 'seitan' to complex recipies such as 'plantain coated sea bass with mango wine sauce') to calculate meals carbohydrates. Therefore, since covering all possible combinations of ingredients and recipes is almost impossible, the ability to learn new food names during the interaction improves user experience.

Linguistic Alignment corresponds to the conversational agent functionality of adapting its language to that of the user. The agent will start using the user's frequent expressions in order to align its lexicon. For example, it should align its linguistic register or reuse the same words used by the user in the generation of the following turn (Branigan et al., 2010; Duplessis et al., 2017).

In Table 1 we give, as an example, the transcript used as stimulus material for the *empathy* variable.

4.2 Dependent Variables

The variables that we adopted in our framework for evaluating QoS and QoE are: (i) **utility**: if the user found the system useful to achieve the task and obtained all the information s/he needed; (ii) **ease of use**: if the system was intuitive in the usage and the user could use it without effort; (iii) **satisfaction**: if the user had a good experience and would use the system again; (iv) **interaction**: if the user appreciated the manner of interacting of the system. The evaluation of these variables has been obtained asking the subjects to choose the interaction that better matched each of the four questions under each interaction pair. According to the kind of system that has to be evaluated, different or more fine grained dependent variables can be chosen. For example, the *cognitive workload* or *effort* perceived by the user, the *appeal* of the interface design or the communication channel.

4.3 Experiment description

In this section we describe the main characteristics of our evaluation experiment.

Subjects: 143 subjects from the US were recruited using the CrowdFlower platform: 93 male and 50 female. 36 were between 18-24 years old, 58 were between 25-34 years old, 31 were between 35-49 years old, 18 were 50 or more aged.

Design: The design was completely within-subject, i.e. each subject was presented with one of the control and experimental transcripts for the 5 variables. Transcripts order among variables and between control/experimental conditions was randomized in order to avoid any framing effect or stimulus order effect (Kessler and Meier, 2014).

Quality control: all subjects were level 3 contributors (maximum expertise/reliability) and a minimum of 3 minutes was set to accept the responses to the questionnaire. No "gold-standard" item was used to evaluate rater reliability, as the two former controls proved to be enough for our case, as found in post hoc analysis.

CH1:	Hello Andrea! What did you eat for your last meal?	CH1:	Hello Andrea! What did you eat for your last meal?
User:	I ate a plate of spaghetti with tomato	User:	I ate a plate of spaghetti with tomato
CH1:	How much spaghetti with tomato did you eat?	CH1:	How much spaghetti with tomato did you eat?
User:	Unfortunately I messed up, it was a generous helping...	User:	Unfortunately I messed up, it was a generous helping...
CH1:	Your meal consisting of a generous plate (200g) of spaghetti with tomato corresponds to 30.85 g of carbohydrates. I hope I have been helpful! See you soon!	CH1:	**Don't worry about it, everyone messes up sometimes!** Anyway, your meal consisting of a generous plate (200g) of spaghetti with tomato corresponds to 30.85 g of carbohydrates. I hope I have been helpful! See you soon!

Table 1: Control (on the left) and experimental (on the right) transcript for the *empathy* independent variable. Portions of CH1 utterances that were changed in order to realize the variable are in bold.

	Ease	Satisf.	Util.	Inter.	Marginal
alignment	0.60	0.61	0.67	0.65	0.63
empathy	0.73	0.78	0.73	0.76	0.75
facing	0.64	0.71	0.70	0.66	0.68
formal	0.74	0.80	0.73	0.66	0.73
vocabulary	0.74	0.71	0.73	0.77	0.74

Table 2: Ratio of subjects that preferred the experimental over the control condition.

	FEMALE	MALE
alignment	**0.68**	**0.61**
empathy	0.77	0.74
facing	0.76	**0.64**
formal	0.76	0.72
vocabulary	0.72	0.75

Table 3: Marginals for the interaction variables according to gender.

Judgments collected: the total number of judgments collected is 2860: 143 subjects that answered four questions for each of the 5 independent variables.

Cost: Overall, the experiment cost was 51.48\$ resulting in a cost of roughly 10\$ for evaluating each variable. The duration of the experiment was about 12 hours. As a side note, the experiment got a high feedback in terms of contributor satisfaction (an overall evaluation of 4.8/5).

4.4 Results

In this section we briefly discuss the results, reported in Table 2, of our pilot experiments. We focus on the ability of our framework to elicit in users' responses a difference between the two levels of each independent variable in terms of perceived QoS and QoE. Results were in line with our expectations: the methodology was able to capture the effect of each modality and strategy of interaction in the experimental condition.

Results shows, indeed, that the contributors expressed a preference for the experimental condition, resulting in a consistent trend with respect to the variables[2]. All results are statistically significant, χ^2 test used. Moreover, the independent variables have different magnitude effects (i.e. some

modalities of interaction were appreciated more). In particular, considering marginals, *empathy*, *formality* and *vocabulary* were the most appreciated variations of CH1 (with no statistical significant difference among them) while *alignment* and *facing* were less appreciated. Interestingly, an analysis at the gender level (see Table 3), revealed that on the two latter variables there was a clear discrepancy in the marginals between male and female: this difference in the case of *alignment* is 0.68 for female vs. 0.61 for male - and both account for the difference in overall results with regard to other independent variables. Instead, for *facing*, the difference in marginals with regard to other independent variables was due to the male group alone, since for female the results are in line with other variables (0.64 vs. 0.76).

Turning to dependent variables we can see that the effect is quite different: *alignment* has a main impact on utility and interaction, *empathy* on satisfaction and interaction, *facing* on satisfaction and utility, *formality* on satisfaction and ease of use, *vocabulary* on naturalness and ease of use. Interestingly each of the independent variables had a main effect on one QoS and one QoE dimension - in line with the findings of (Jurčíček et al., 2011).

4.5 Comparison with WoZ

Finally, we simulated a WoZ experiment in order to compare the design, implementation and performance of our framework. While the instruction

---

[2]Actually, for the formal/informal dimension the preference went to the control condition (formal register). Still, for comparability purposes we report results for the control condition in Table 2

and stimuli creation require in both cases almost the same time (for example the stimulus material for our setting was used as an example of possible interaction for the Wizard instructions), the implementation of our framework is much faster. Indeed, the WoZ experiment requires the implementation of a graphical user interface, but even if we use a pre-set one, we still need to instruct Wizard(s) and find a relevant number of participants in case a crowdsourcing methodology is not used. But even if we do not consider the aforementioned time consuming preparatory activities, each WoZ session that replicate our experiment, required 30 minutes and two participants, as compared to the 3 minutes and one participant required by our framework. This is explained by the fact that while in our framework the subject just need to read the transcript of the interaction, in the WoZ experiment the user needs to read instructions for each interaction, think and digit the input at each turn and read the corresponding wizard response; at the same time the Wizard needs to do the same.

5 Advantages

With the initial evidence, provided by the experiments, we can reasonably state that the framework we are proposing has some important advantages:

Cheap and Fast. The evaluation can be obtained using platform such as CrowdFlower or AMT, choosing high level and possibly native speaker contributors. Crowdsourcing approaches make it quick and cheap to run evaluation experiments as compared to ecological ones, see for example what reported in (Reiter, 2011).

Flexibility. The framework gives the possibility to define the dependent and independent variables that better match the strategies and modalities of interaction that need to be evaluated. Moreover, using crowdsourcing approaches together with hand curated transcripts we can easily experiment several variables/versions of the conversational agents or control for multiple mixed effects (e.g. linguistic style * empathy). We can also test different levels of a strategy, for example to find the optimal formality level.

Experiment design. the adoption of a pairwise comparison of the two versions of the system makes the evaluation of the interaction strategies faster and more direct. It also halves the number of judgments required with respect to traditional evaluation designs in which each stimulus material is served separatedly, bringing to an approximative halving of the price.

Control over the variables being tested. Providing transcripts of the conversation to the subjects gives the possibility to control one variable at a time isolating its effect (and to the best of our knowledge no previous work ever tried this approach). This allow us, for example, to build transcripts with an almost equal number of tokens and turns of interactions, in order to avoid phenomena such as length effect (Koizumi, 2012).

Judgement Elicitation. Forcing a choice between control and experimental condition allows eliciting possible differences between the two interactions, for how small this difference could be.

Effort Reduction. Since the subjects of the experiment are not meant to interact directly with the conversational agent, we can create an off-line experiment to test conversational agents characteristics in advance, rather than having a post-process analysis. This saves implementation or data collection effort, since there might be aspects of the interaction that annoy the user or, on the contrary, that have a positive impact and that are easy to implement. Finally, we can avoid the risk that the user could miss some passages of the interaction useful to highlight the strategies that we are analyzing, as could happen in WoZ studies.

6 Conclusion and Future Works

In our view, the proposed framework, based on a pairwise comparison of manually curated and controlled transcripts, represents a step forward in the evaluation of dialogue systems. This methodology allows evaluating the strategies and the interaction modalities of a conversational agent before its implementation, ensuring the advantages reported above. We believe that this methodology is suitable not only for rule-based systems, but also for data-driven ones. In this latter case the methodology can be used, for example, to define the constraints for data collection.

In future works, we would like to define and test other strategies of interaction, but it might be necessary - to create proper transcripts - to define new guidelines and parameters. For example if a strategy involves choosing between two different dialog paths (i.e. several turns might change) the guidelines on insertion or substitution we defined are not sufficient.

References

Enrique Alfonseca. 2017. Evaluation of speech for the google assistant. *https://ai.googleblog.com/2017/12/evaluation-of-speech-for-google.html*.

James F Allen, Donna K Byron, Myroslava Dzikovska, George Ferguson, Lucian Galescu, and Amanda Stent. 2001. Toward conversational human-computer interaction. *AI magazine*, 22(4):27.

Alexandra Balahur, Rada Mihalcea, and Andrés Montoyo. 2014. Computational approaches to subjectivity and sentiment analysis: Present and envisaged methods and applications.

Lisa Feldman Barrett, Kristen A Lindquist, and Maria Gendron. 2007. Language as context for the perception of emotion. *Trends in cognitive sciences*, 11(8):327–332.

Ondrej Bojar, Rajen Chatterjee, Christian Federmann, Yvette Graham, Barry Haddow, Matthias Huck, Antonio Jimeno Yepes, Philipp Koehn, Varvara Logacheva, Christof Monz, et al. 2016. Findings of the 2016 conference on machine translation. In *ACL 2016 FIRST CONFERENCE ON MACHINE TRANSLATION (WMT16)*, pages 131–198. The Association for Computational Linguistics.

Kevin K Bowden, Shereen Oraby, Amita Misra, Jiaqi Wu, and Stephanie Lukin. 2017. Data-driven dialogue systems for social agents. *arXiv preprint arXiv:1709.03190*.

Holly P Branigan, Martin J Pickering, Jamie Pearson, and Janet F McLean. 2010. Linguistic alignment between people and computers. *Journal of Pragmatics*, 42(9):2355–2368.

Julian Brooke, Tong Wang, and Graeme Hirst. 2010. Automatic acquisition of lexical formality. In *Proceedings of the 23rd International Conference on Computational Linguistics: Posters*, pages 90–98. Association for Computational Linguistics.

Zoraida Callejas, David Griol, and Ramón López-Cózar. 2011. Predicting user mental states in spoken dialogue systems. *EURASIP Journal on Advances in Signal Processing*, 2011(1):6.

Amanda Cercas Curry, Helen Hastie, and Verena Rieser. 2017. A review of evaluation techniques for social dialogue systems. *arXiv preprint arXiv:1709.04409*.

Yun-Nung Chen, William Yang Wang, and Alexander I Rudnicky. 2013. Unsupervised induction and filling of semantic slots for spoken dialogue systems using frame-semantic parsing. In *Automatic Speech Recognition and Understanding (ASRU), 2013 IEEE Workshop on*, pages 120–125. IEEE.

Aleksandr Chuklin, Aliaksei Severyn, Johanne Trippas, Enrique Alfonseca, Hanna Silen, and Damiano Spina. 2018. Prosody modifications for question-answering in voice-only settings. *arXiv preprint arXiv:1806.03957*.

Nils Dahlbäck, Arne Jönsson, and Lars Ahrenberg. 1993. Wizard of oz studies - why and how. *Knowledge-based systems*, 6(4):258–266.

Guillaume Dubuisson Duplessis, Chloé Clavel, and Frédéric Landragin. 2017. Automatic measures to characterise verbal alignment in human-agent interaction. In *18th Annual Meeting of the Special Interest Group on Discourse and Dialogue (SIGDIAL)*, pages 71–81.

Laila Dybkjaer, Niels Ole Bernsen, and Wolfgang Minker. 2004. Evaluation and usability of multimodal spoken language dialogue systems. *Speech Communication*, 43(1-2):33–54.

Matthew Frampton and Oliver Lemon. 2006. Learning more effective dialogue strategies using limited dialogue move features. In *Proceedings of the 21st International Conference on Computational Linguistics and the 44th annual meeting of the Association for Computational Linguistics*, pages 185–192. Association for Computational Linguistics.

Yvette Graham, Timothy Baldwin, Alistair Moffat, and Justin Zobel. 2013. Continuous measurement scales in human evaluation of machine translation. In *Proceedings of the 7th Linguistic Annotation Workshop and Interoperability with Discourse*, pages 33–41.

Marco Guerini, Carlo Strapparava, and Oliviero Stock. 2012. Ecological evaluation of persuasive messages using google adwords. In *Proceedings of the 50th Annual Meeting of the Association for Computational Linguistics: Long Papers-Volume 1*, pages 988–996. Association for Computational Linguistics.

Francis Heylighen and Jean-Marc Dewaele. 1999. Formality of language: definition, measurement and behavioral determinants.

Filip Jurčíček, Simon Keizer, Milica Gašić, Francois Mairesse, Blaise Thomson, Kai Yu, and Steve Young. 2011. Real user evaluation of spoken dialogue systems using amazon mechanical turk. In *Twelfth Annual Conference of the International Speech Communication Association*.

Judd B Kessler and Stephan Meier. 2014. Learning from (failed) replications: Cognitive load manipulations and charitable giving. *Journal of Economic Behavior & Organization*, 102:10–13.

Rie Koizumi. 2012. Relationships between text length and lexical diversity measures: Can we use short texts of less than 100 tokens. *Vocabulary Learning and Instruction*, 1(1):60–69.

Esther Levin and Roberto Pieraccini. 1997. A stochastic model of computer-human interaction for learning dialogue strategies. In *Fifth European Conference on Speech Communication and Technology*.

Chia-Wei Liu, Ryan Lowe, Iulian V Serban, Michael Noseworthy, Laurent Charlin, and Joelle Pineau. 2016. How not to evaluate your dialogue system: An empirical study of unsupervised evaluation metrics for dialogue response generation. *arXiv preprint arXiv:1603.08023*.

MO Meira and AMP Canuto. 2015. Evaluation of emotional agents' architectures: an approach based on quality metrics and the influence of emotions on users. In *Proceedings of the World Congress on Engineering*, volume 1.

Sebastian Moller, Klaus-Peter Engelbrecht, Christine Kuhnel, Ina Wechsung, and Benjamin Weiss. 2009. A taxonomy of quality of service and quality of experience of multimodal human-machine interaction. In *Quality of Multimedia Experience, 2009. QoMEx 2009. International Workshop on*, pages 7–12. IEEE.

Kellie Morrissey and Jurek Kirakowski. 2013. In *International Conference on Human-Computer Interaction*, pages 87–96. Springer.

Tim Paek. 2001. Empirical methods for evaluating dialog systems. In *Proceedings of the workshop on Evaluation for Language and Dialogue Systems-Volume 9*, page 2. Association for Computational Linguistics.

Louisa Pragst, Wolfgang Minker, and Stefan Ultes. 2017. Exploring the applicability of elaborateness and indirectness in dialogue management.

Nicole M Radziwill and Morgan C Benton. 2017. Evaluating quality of chatbots and intelligent conversational agents. *arXiv preprint arXiv:1704.04579*.

Antoine Raux, Dan Bohus, Brian Langner, Alan W Black, and Maxine Eskenazi. 2006. Doing research on a deployed spoken dialogue system: One year of let's go! experience. In *Ninth International Conference on Spoken Language Processing*.

Ehud Reiter. 2011. Task-based evaluation of nlg systems: Control vs real-world context. In *Proceedings of the UCNLG+ Eval: Language Generation and Evaluation Workshop*, pages 28–32. Association for Computational Linguistics.

Giuseppe Riccardi and Dilek Hakkani-Tur. 2005. Active learning: Theory and applications to automatic speech recognition. *IEEE transactions on speech and audio processing*, 13(4):504–511.

Stefan Riezler, Tracy H King, Richard Crouch, and Annie Zaenen. 2003. Statistical sentence condensation using ambiguity packing and stochastic disambiguation methods for lexical-functional grammar. In *Proceedings of the 2003 Conference of the North American Chapter of the Association for Computational Linguistics on Human Language Technology-Volume 1*, pages 118–125. Association for Computational Linguistics.

Oscar J Romero, Ran Zhao, and Justine Cassell. 2017. Cognitive-inspired conversational-strategy reasoner for socially-aware agents. In *Proceedings of the 26th International Joint Conference on Artificial Intelligence*, pages 3807–3813. AAAI Press.

Konrad Scheffler and Steve Young. 2002. Automatic learning of dialogue strategy using dialogue simulation and reinforcement learning. In *Proceedings of the second international conference on Human Language Technology Research*, pages 12–19. Morgan Kaufmann Publishers Inc.

Björn Schuller, Stefan Steidl, Anton Batliner, Alessandro Vinciarelli, Klaus Scherer, Fabien Ringeval, Mohamed Chetouani, Felix Weninger, Florian Eyben, Erik Marchi, et al. 2013. The interspeech 2013 computational paralinguistics challenge: social signals, conflict, emotion, autism. In *Proceedings INTERSPEECH 2013, 14th Annual Conference of the International Speech Communication Association, Lyon, France*.

Bayan Abu Shawar and Eric Atwell. 2007. Different measurements metrics to evaluate a chatbot system. In *Proceedings of the workshop on bridging the gap: Academic and industrial research in dialog technologies*, pages 89–96. Association for Computational Linguistics.

Annika Silvervarg and Arne Jönsson. 2011. Subjective and objective evaluation of conversational agents in learning environments for young teenagers. In *Proceedings of the 7th IJCAI Workshop on Knowledge and Reasoning in Practical Dialogue Systems*.

Gabriel Skantze. 2005. Exploring human error recovery strategies: Implications for spoken dialogue systems. *Speech Communication*, 45(3):325–341.

Chenhao Tan, Lillian Lee, and Bo Pang. 2014. The effect of wording on message propagation: Topic- and author-controlled natural experiments on twitter. *arXiv preprint arXiv:1405.1438*.

Johanne R Trippas, Damiano Spina, Lawrence Cavedon, and Mark Sanderson. 2017. Crowdsourcing user preferences and ery judgments for speech-only search. In *1st SIGIR Workshop on Conversational Approaches to Information Retrieval (CAIR'17)*.

Ielka Van Der Sluis and Chris Mellish. 2010. Towards empirical evaluation of affective tactical nlg. In *Empirical methods in natural language generation*, pages 242–263. Springer.

Marilyn A Walker, Diane J Litman, Candace A Kamm, and Alicia Abella. 1997. Paradise: A framework for evaluating spoken dialogue agents. In *Proceedings of the eighth conference on European chapter of the Association for Computational Linguistics*, pages 271–280. Association for Computational Linguistics.

Tsung-Hsien Wen, Milica Gasic, Nikola Mrksic, Pei-Hao Su, David Vandyke, and Steve Young. 2015. Semantically conditioned lstm-based natural language generation for spoken dialogue systems. *arXiv preprint arXiv:1508.01745*.

Tsung-Hsien Wen, David Vandyke, Nikola Mrksic, Milica Gasic, Lina M Rojas-Barahona, Pei-Hao Su, Stefan Ultes, and Steve Young. 2016. A network-based end-to-end trainable task-oriented dialogue system. *arXiv preprint arXiv:1604.04562*.

Zhaojun Yang, Baichuan Li, Yi Zhu, Irwin King, Gina Levow, and Helen Meng. 2010. Collection of user judgments on spoken dialog system with crowdsourcing. In *Spoken Language Technology Workshop (SLT), 2010 IEEE*, pages 277–282. IEEE.

A Reinforcement Learning-driven Translation Model for Search-Oriented Conversational Systems

Wafa Aissa
Sorbonne Université
CNRS, LIP6
F-75005 Paris, France
wafa.aissa@lip6.fr

Laure Soulier
Sorbonne Université
CNRS, LIP6
F-75005 Paris, France
laure.soulier@lip6.fr

Ludovic Denoyer
Sorbonne Université
CNRS, LIP6
F-75005 Paris, France
ludovic.denoyer@lip6.fr

Abstract

Search-oriented conversational systems rely on information needs expressed in natural language (NL). We focus here on the understanding of NL expressions for building keyword-based queries. We propose a reinforcement-learning-driven translation model framework able to 1) learn the translation from NL expressions to queries in a supervised way, and, 2) to overcome the lack of large-scale dataset by framing the translation model as a word selection approach and injecting relevance feedback as a reward in the learning process. Experiments are carried out on two TREC datasets. We outline the effectiveness of our approach.

1 Introduction

Artificial Intelligence, and more particularly deep learning, have recently opened tremendous perspectives for reasoning over semantics in text-based applications such as machine translation (Lample et al., 2017), chat-bot (Bordes and Weston, 2016), knowledge base completion (Lin et al., 2015) or extraction (Hoffmann et al., 2011). Very recently, conversational information retrieval (IR) has emerged as a new paradigm in IR (Burtsev et al., 2017; Joho et al., 2018), in which natural conversations between humans and computers are used to satisfy an information need. As for now, conversational systems are limited to simple conversational interactions (namely, chit-chat conversations) (Li et al., 2016; Ritter et al., 2011), closed worlds driven by domain-adapted or slot-filling patterns (Bordes and Weston, 2016; Wang and Lemon, 2013) (e.g., a travel planning task requiring to book a flight, then a hotel, etc...), or knowledge-base extraction (e.g., information extraction tasks) (Dhingra et al., 2017).

In contrast, search-oriented conversational systems (SOCS) aim at finding information in an open world (both unstructured information sources and knowledge-bases) in response to users' information needs expressed in natural language (NL); the latter often being ambiguous. Therefore, one key challenge of SOCS is to understand users' information needs expressed in NL to identify relevant documents.

Formulating an information need through queries has been outlined as a difficult task (Vakulenko et al., 2017; Agichtein et al., 2006; Joachims, 2002) which is generally tackled by refining/reformulating queries using pseudo-relevance feedback or users' clicks. In SOCS, there is an upstream challenge dealing with the building of the query from a NL expression that initiates the search session to avoid useless users' interactions with the system. This problem could be tackled for instance through deep neural translation models (e.g., encoder-decoder approaches) as initiated by (Song et al., 2017; Yin et al., 2017). However, these methods learn the query formulation model independently of the search task at hand. To overpass this limitation, (Nogueira and Cho, 2017) have proposed a reinforcement learning model for query reformulation in which the reward is based on terms of documents retrieved by the IR system.

In this work, we propose to bridge these two lines of work: 1) machine translation to learn the mapping between information needs expressed in NL and information needs formulated using keywords (Song et al., 2017; Yin et al., 2017), and 2) reinforcement learning to inject the task objectives within the machine translation model (Nogueira and Cho, 2017). More particularly, we propose a two-step model which first learns the translation model through the supervision of NL-query pairs and then refines the translation model using a relevance feedback provided by

Proceedings of the 2018 EMNLP Workshop SCAI: The 2nd Int'l Workshop on Search-Oriented Conversational AI, pages 33–39
Brussels, Belgium, October 31, 2018. ©2018 Association for Computational Linguistics

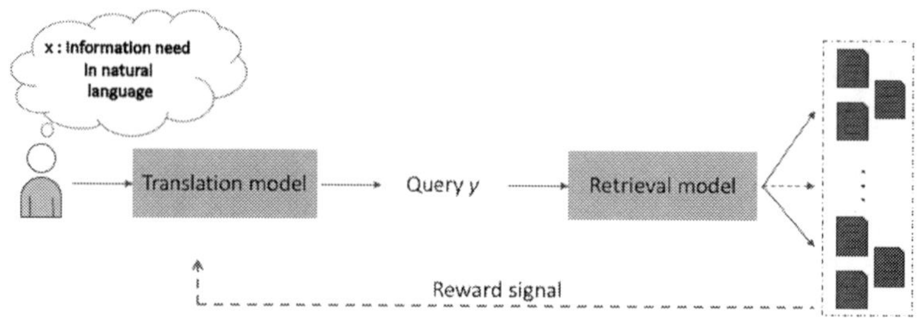

Figure 1: Overview of our reinforcement learning-driven translation model for SOCS

the search engine. It is worth mentioning that there does not exist SOCS-oriented dataset that both aligns users' information needs in NL with keyword-based queries and includes a document collection to perform a retrieval task. To the best of our knowledge, TREC datasets are the only ones expressing such constraint, but the number of NL-query pairs is however limited. To fit with the issue of dealing with large vocabulary and the dataset constraint, we frame the translation model as a word selection one which aims at identifying which words in the NL expression can be used to build the query. Our model is evaluated on two TREC datasets. The obtained results outline the effectiveness of combining reinforcement learning with machine translation models.

The remaining of the paper is organized as follows. Section 2 details our translation model. Section 3 presents the evaluation protocol and results are highlighted in Section 4. The conclusion and perspectives are discussed in Section 5.

2 Reinforcement learning-driven translation model

2.1 Notation and problem formulation

Our reinforcement learning-driven translation model allows to formulate a user's information need x expressed in NL into a keyword-based query y. The user's information need x is a sequence of n words ($x = x_1, ..., x_i, ..., x_n$). To fit with our word selection objective, the query y is modeled as a binary vector $y \in \{0,1\}^n$ of size n (namely, the size of the natural language expression x). Each element $y_j \in y$ equals to 1 if word $x_i \in x$ exists in query y and 0 otherwise. For example, if we consider the NL as "Identify documents that discuss sick building syndrome or building related illnesses." and

the key-words query as "sick building syndrome.", the expected query will be formulated as follows:
$y = (0, 0, 0, 0, 1, 1, 1, 0, 0, 0, 0)$.

The objective of our model f_θ (with θ being the parameters of our model) is to estimate the probability $p(y|x)$ of generating the binary vector y given the NL expression x. Since terms are not independent within the formulation of NL expressions and queries, it makes sense to consider that the selection of a word is conditioned by the sequence of decisions taken on previous words $y_{<i}$. Thus, $P(y|x)$ could be written as follows:

$$p(y|x) = \prod_{y_i \in y} p(y_i|y_{<i}, x) \qquad (1)$$

This probability is first learned using a maximum likelihood estimation (MLE) on the basis of NL-query pairs (Section 2.2). Then, this probability is refined using reinforcement learning techniques (Section 2.3). We end up with the network architecture used in the translation model.

2.2 Supervised translation model: from NL to queries

The translation model works as a supervised word selection model aiming at building queries y by using the vocabulary available in NL expressions x. To do so, we use a set D of N NL-query pairs $D = \{(x^1, y^1), ..., (x^k, y^k), ..., (x^N, y^N)\}$.

The objective of the translation model is to predict whether each word x_i^k in the NL expression x^k is included in the expected query y^k. In other words, it consists in predicting the probability $p(\hat{y}_i^k = y_i^k|\hat{y}_{<i}^k, x^k)$ that the ith element $\hat{y}_i^k$ of vector $\hat{y}^k$ is equal to the same element y_i^k in the original query y^k (namely, that $\hat{y}_i^k = y_i^k$) given the state of previous elements $\hat{y}_{<i}^k$ and the NL expression x^k. This probability $p(\hat{y}_i^k = y_i^k|\hat{y}_{<i}^k, x^k)$ is modeled using a Bernoulli distribution in which parameters are estimated through the probability distribution.

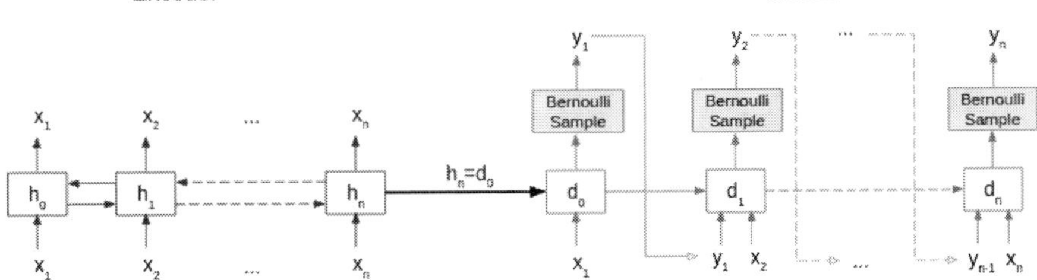

Figure 2: Network architecture of our translation model

Let's define for a NL-query instance (x^k, y^k), $f_{(\theta, x^k)} = \sum_{y_i^k \in y^k} log(p(\hat{y}_i^k = y_i^k | \hat{y}_{<i}^k, x^k))$. The translation model is trained by maximizing the following MLE over the set D of NL-query pairs (x_k, y_k):

$$L_{SMT} = \sum_{(x^k, y^k) \in D} log(f(\theta, x^k)) \quad (2)$$

2.3 Reinforcement learning

To inject the task objective in the translation model, we consider that the process of query building could be enhanced through reinforcement learning techniques. Therefore, the word selection could be seen as a sequence of choices of selecting word x_t at each time step t. The choices are *rewarded* at the end of the selection process by a metric measuring the effectiveness of the query building process within a retrieval task. Particularly, the predicted query $\hat{y}$ obtained from the binary vector $\hat{y}$ is fed to a retrieval model to rank documents. For each NL expression x (and accordingly the associated predicted query $\hat{y}$), we dispose of a set $\mathcal{D}_x$ of relevant documents (also called ground truth). We note GT the set of n pairs $(x; \mathcal{D}_x)$. With this in mind, the effectiveness of the obtained ranking could be estimated using an effectiveness-driven metric (e.g., the MAP). Thus, the reward R for a generated query $\hat{y}$ given the relevance feedback pair $(x, \mathcal{D}_x)$ is obtained as follows:

$$R(\hat{y}) = MAP(\hat{y}, \mathcal{D}_x) \quad (3)$$

At the end of the selection process, the objective function aims at maximizing the expectation of the search effectiveness over the predicted queries:

$$L_{RL}(\theta) = arg \max_{\theta} \; \mathbb{E}_{\substack{(x; \mathcal{D}_x) \in GT \\ \hat{y} \sim f_\theta(x)}} [R(\hat{y})] \quad (4)$$

where $\hat{y}$ is given by the translation model $f_\theta(x)$. This objective function is maximized using gradient descent techniques (Baxter et al., 1999).

2.4 Model architecture

The model is based on an encoder-decoder building a query $\hat{q}$ from the input x. Particularly, each element x_i of x is modeled through word embeddings w_{x_i}; resulting in a sequence w_x of word embeddings for input x. As shown in Figure 2, the encoder is a bi-directional LSTM (Hochreiter and Schmidhuber, 1997) aiming to transform the input sequence w_x to its continuous representation h_n. The decoder is composed of a LSTM in which each word x_i is injected to estimate the word selection probability $p(y_i | y_{<i}, x)$ using the hidden vector h_n learned in the encoder network and the current word x_i; leading to estimate probability $p(y_i | y_{<i}, x_i, h_n)$.

3 Protocol design

3.1 Datasets

Since there does not exist yet SOCS-driven datasets including NL-query pairs, we use TREC tracks (namely, Robust 2004 and Web 2000-2001). In these tracks, query topics include a title, a topic description and a narrative text; the two latter being formulated in natural language. To build query-NL pairs, we use the title to form the set of keyword queries and the description for the set of information needs expressed in NL. An example of a query-NL pair is:

Title	Lewis and Clark expedition
Description	What are some useful sites containing information about the historic Lewis and Clark expedition?

This NL-query building process results in 350 pairs in total as presented in Table 1.

We are aware that the use of TREC datasets is biased in the sense that it does not exactly fit with the expression of NL information need in the context of conversational systems, but we believe that the description is enough verbose to evaluate the impact of our query building model in this ex-

35

TREC track	collection	pairs	NL length	avg of duplic. word in NL
TREC Robust (2004)	disk4-5	250	15.333	1.108
TREC Web (2000 2001)	WT10G	100	11.47	0.65

Table 1: Dataset statistics separated per document collections

ploratory work. Further experiments with generated datasets, as done in (Song et al., 2017), will be carried out in the future.

We also analyze the issue of duplicate words into TREC descriptions since it can directly impact the query formulation process based on word selection in the word sequence of TREC descriptions. In practice, this might lead to select several times the same word to build the query, and, therefore, directly impact the retrieval performance. As shown in Table 1, the ratio of duplicate words in TREC descriptions over the whole set of queries is very low (1.1 duplicate words in average in each query for TREC Robust and 0.65 for TREC Web). This suggests that this issue is minor in the used datasets. We, therefore, decided to skip this issue for the moment.

3.2 Metrics and baselines

To evaluate our approach, we measure the retrieval effectiveness of the predicted queries. To do so, for each predicted query, we run the BM25 model through an IR system (namely, PyLucene[1]) to obtain a document ranking. The latter is evaluated through the MAP metric.

To show the soundness of our approach (namely, translating information needs expressed in NL into queries), we compare our generated queries to scenario **NL** feeding the natural language information needs (TREC descriptions in our protocol) to the IR retrieval system.

Since the objective of our model is to formulate queries, we also evaluate the effectiveness of original TREC titles (scenario **Q**). This setting rather refers to the oracle that our model must reach.

We mentioned that before training the selection model we transformed each x to its binary representation y based on the presence of the words in the ground truth query. The dataset being slightly biased by this binary modeling, we observed that not all the words existing in the query do exist in x. To analyze this bias, we also compare our approach with these binary queries (scenario **Q bin**)

referring to the projection of queries **Q** on the vocabulary available in the **NL** description.

We also compare our model to a random approach which randomly selects 3 words from x to build queries (scenario **Random**).

Different variants of our model are also tested:

- **SMT** which only considers the first component of our model based on a supervised machine translation approach (Section 2.2). This variant could be assimilated to the approach proposed in (Song et al., 2017) in the sense that the machine translation is performed independently of the task objective.

- **RL** which only considers the reinforcement learning objective function (Section 2.3) without pre-training of the supervised translation model.

- **SMT+RL** which is our full model in which we start by pre-training the model using the supervised translation model (Section 2.3), and, then, we inject the reward signal in the translation probabilities (Section 2.4).

3.3 Implementation details

To transform each word x_i to its vector representation w_{x_i}, we use Fasttext [2] (Bojanowski et al., 2017) pre-trained word embeddings. The encoder and decoders have one hidden layer with 100 hidden units each.

To train our model, we perform 10-fold cross-validation. For the **SMT+RL** model, we start by a pre-training using the supervised translation model for 100 iterations. The training is then pursued by 1000 iterations while including the reinforcement learning approach. In the latter, the reward, namely the MAP metric, is estimated over document rankings obtained by the BM25 model in PyLucene. We use a minibatch Adam (Kingma and Ba, 2014) algorithm to pre-train the model and SGD for the reinforcement learning part. Each update is computed after a minibatch of 12 sentences.

---

[1] http://lucene.apache.org/pylucene/

[2] https://github.com/facebookresearch/fastText/

Baseline	TREC Robust(2004)		TREC Web (2000-2001)	
	MAP	%Chg	MAP	%Chg
NL	0.08925	+15.25% ***	0.15913	+12.88% *
Q	0.09804	+4.92%	0.16543	+8.58%
Q bin	0.08847	+16.26% *	0.17402	+3.22%
Random	0.01808	+468.91% ***	0.04060	+342.44% ***
SMT	0.06845	+50.27% ***	0.08891	+102.04% ***
RL	0.08983	+14.51% ***	0.16474	+9.04%
SMT+RL	**0.10286**		**0.17963**	

Table 2: Comparative effectiveness analysis of our approach. $\%Chg$: improvement of **SMT+RL** over corresponding baselines. Paired t-test significance *: $0.01 < t \leq 0.05$; **: $0.001 < t \leq 0.01$; ***: $t \leq 0.001$.

NL	Q	Q bin	SMT+RL
what are new methods of producing steel	steel producing	producing steel	new methods of producing steel
what are the advantages and or disadvantages of tooth implant	implant dentistry	implant	advantages disadvantages tooth implant
find documents that discuss the toronto film festival awards	toronto film awards	toronto film awards	the toronto film festival awards
find documents that give growth rates of pine trees	where can i find growth rates for the pine trees	growth rates pine trees	growth rates of pine trees

Table 3: Examples of query formulation for **NL** queries, the original query **Q**, the binary version **Q bin** of the original query, and our model **SMT+RL**.

4   Results

We present here the effectiveness of our approach aiming at generating queries from users' information needs expressed in NL. In Table 2, we present the retrieval effectiveness (regarding the MAP) of our model and the different baselines (**NL**, **Q**, **Q bin**, **Random**, **SMT**, and **RL**) described in section 3.2. From a general point of view, results highlight that in both datasets, our proposed model **SMT+RL** outperforms the different baselines with improvements that are generally significant, ranging from $+3.22\%$ to $+468.91\%$.

More particularly, the effectiveness analysis allows to draw the following statements:

• The overall performance of the compared approaches generally outperforms the retrieval effectiveness of the **NL** baseline. For instance, on TREC Robust, queries generated by our model allows to significantly improve the retrieval performance of $+15.25\%$ regarding information needs expressed in NL (MAP: 0.10286 vs. 0.08925). This result validates the motivation of this work to formulate queries from NL expressions. This is relatively intuitive since NL expressions are verbose by nature and might include non-specific words willing to inject noise in the retrieval process.

• Our approach **SMT+RL** provides similar results as the **Q** and **Q bin**. Since the objective function of our model is guided by the initial query **Q** transformed in a binary vector (**Q bin**), these baselines could be considered as oracles. We note however that our model obtains higher results (improvements from $+3.22\%$ to $+16.26\%$) with a significant difference for the **Q bin** baseline for TREC Robust. To get a better understanding to what extent our generated queries are different from those used in baselines **Q** and **Q bin**, we illustrate in Table 3 some examples. While queries in **Q** identify the most important words leading to an exploratory query (e.g. "steel productions"), our model **SMT+RL** provides additional words that precise which facet of the query is concerned (e.g., "new methods of..."), and accordingly improves the ranking of documents.

• Our model **SMT+RL** is significantly higher than the **SMT** baseline which converges to a relatively low MAP value (0.06845 and 0.08891 for TREC Robust and TREC Web, respectively). This could be explained by the fact that our datasets are very small (250 and 100 NL-query pairs respectively for TREC Robust and TREC Web) and that such machine translation approaches are well-known to be data hungry. Reinforcement learning techniques could be a solution to overpass this problem since they inject additional information (namely, the reward) in the network learning.

- The **RL** baseline achieves relatively good retrieval performances. As we can see from TREC Web, the **RL** model obtains a MAP of 0.16474 against 0.15913 for the **NL** baseline. The **RL** baseline allows approaching the retrieval performances of baselines **Q** and **Q bin**, although it obtains lower results. This reinforces our intuition that 1) applying machine translation approaches should be driven by the task (retrieval task in our context) and 2) reinforcement learning techniques provide good strategies to build effective queries. The latter statement has also been outlined in previous work (Nogueira and Cho, 2017).

- The comparison of our model **SMT+RL** regarding **SMT** and **RL** baselines outlines that reinforcement learning techniques might be more beneficial when a pre-training is performed. In our context, the pre-training is performed using the **SMT** model (Section 2.3) which helps the model to be more general and effective before using the reward signal to guide the selection process.

It is worth mentioning that we also trained in preliminary experiments a state of the art translation models such as a generative encoder-decoder RNN with attention mechanism, as done in (Yin et al., 2017; Song et al., 2017). We did not report the results since the model was not able to generalize in the testing phase over new samples from the NL-query dataset used in the training phase. This is probably due to the trade-off between the number of training pairs and the large size of the vocabulary which is not enough represented in different contexts. However, we believe that combining reinforcement learning with attention-mechanism for query-generation is promising. We let this perspective for future work.

5 Conclusion and future work

We propose a selection model to transform user's need in NL into a keyword query to increase the retrieval effectiveness in a SOCS context. Our model bridges two lines of work dealing with supervised machine translation and reinforcement learning. Our model has been evaluated using two different TREC datasets and outlines promising results in terms of effectiveness. Our approach has some limitations we plan to overcome in the future. First, our model is framed as a word selection process that could be turned into a generative model. Second, experiments are carried out on small datasets (250 and 100 NL-query pairs) that could be augmented using the evaluation protocol proposed in (Song et al., 2017). In long term, we plan to adapt our model by totally skipping the query formulation step and designing retrieval models dealing with NL expressions.

References

Eugene Agichtein, Eric Brill, and Susan Dumais. 2006. Improving web search ranking by incorporating user behavior information. In *SIGIR '06*, pages 19–26.

Jonathan Baxter, Lex Weaver, and Peter Bartlett. 1999. Direct gradient-based reinforcement learning: Ii. gradient ascent algorithms and experiments. Technical report, National University.

Piotr Bojanowski, Edouard Grave, Armand Joulin, and Tomas Mikolov. 2017. Enriching word vectors with subword information. *Transactions of the Association for Computational Linguistics*, 5:135–146.

Antoine Bordes and Jason Weston. 2016. Learning end-to-end goal-oriented dialog. *CoRR*, abs/1605.07683.

Mikhail Burtsev, Aleksandr Chuklin, Julia Kiseleva, and Alexey Borisov. 2017. Search-oriented conversational ai (scai). In *ICTIR '17*, pages 333–334. ACM.

Bhuwan Dhingra, Lihong Li, Xiujun Li, Jianfeng Gao, Yun-Nung Chen, Faisal Ahmed, and Li Deng. 2017. Towards end-to-end reinforcement learning of dialogue agents for information access. In *ACL' 17*, pages 484–495.

Sepp Hochreiter and Jürgen Schmidhuber. 1997. Long short-term memory. *Neural Comput.*, 9(8):1735–1780.

Raphael Hoffmann, Congle Zhang, Xiao Ling, Luke Zettlemoyer, and Daniel S. Weld. 2011. Knowledge-based weak supervision for information extraction of overlapping relations. In *HLT '11*, pages 541–550.

Thorsten Joachims. 2002. Optimizing Search Engines Using Clickthrough Data. In *SIGKDD '02*, pages 133–142. ACM.

Hideo Joho, Lawrence Cavedon, Jaime Arguello, Milad Shokouhi, and Filip Radlinski. 2018. Cair'17: First international workshop on conversational approaches to information retrieval at sigir 2017. *SIGIR Forum*, 51(3):114–121.

Diederik P. Kingma and Jimmy Ba. 2014. Adam: A method for stochastic optimization. *CoRR*, abs/1412.6980.

Guillaume Lample, Ludovic Denoyer, and Marc'Aurelio Ranzato. 2017. Unsupervised machine translation using monolingual corpora only. *CoRR*, abs/1711.00043.

Jiwei Li, Michel Galley, Chris Brockett, Jianfeng Gao, and Bill Dolan. 2016. A diversity-promoting objective function for neural conversation models. In *HLT '16*, pages 110–119. ACL.

Yankai Lin, Zhiyuan Liu, Maosong Sun, Yang Liu, and Xuan Zhu. 2015. Learning entity and relation embeddings for knowledge graph completion. In *AAAI*, pages 2181–2187. AAAI Press.

Rodrigo Nogueira and Kyunghyun Cho. 2017. Task-oriented query reformulation with reinforcement learning. In *SCAI Workshop - ICTIR*.

Alan Ritter, Colin Cherry, and William B. Dolan. 2011. Data-driven response generation in social media. In *EMNLP '11*.

Hyun-Je Song, A-Yeong Kim, and Seong-Bae Park. 2017. Translation of natural language query into keyword query using a rnn encoder-decoder. In *SIGIR '17*, pages 965–968.

Svitlana Vakulenko, Ilya Markov, and Maarten de Rijke. 2017. Conversational exploratory search via interactive storytelling. In *NEUIR SIGIR'17*.

Zhuoran Wang and Oliver Lemon. 2013. A simple and generic belief tracking mechanism for the dialog state tracking challenge: On the believability of observed information. In *SIGDIAL' 13*, page 423–432.

Zi Yin, Keng-hao Chang, and Ruofei Zhang. 2017. Deepprobe: Information directed sequence understanding and chatbot design via recurrent neural networks. In *SIGKDD' 17*, pages 2131–2139.

Research Challenges in Building a Voice-based Artificial Personal Shopper - Position Paper

Nut Limsopatham
Amazon Research
Seattle
Washington, USA
`nutli@amazon.com`

Oleg Rokhlenko
Amazon Research
Seattle
Washington, USA
`olegro@amazon.com`

David Carmel
Amazon Research
Matam Park
Haifa, Israel
`david.carmel@gmail.com`

Abstract

Recent advances in automatic speech recognition lead toward enabling a voice conversation between a human user and an intelligent virtual assistant. This provides a potential foundation for developing artificial personal shoppers for e-commerce websites, such as Alibaba, Amazon, and eBay. Personal shoppers are valuable to the on-line shops as they enhance user engagement and trust by promptly dealing with customers' questions and concerns. Developing an artificial personal shopper requires the agent to leverage knowledge about the customer and products, while interacting with the customer in a human-like conversation. In this position paper, we motivate and describe *the artificial personal shopper task*, and then address a research agenda for this task by adapting and advancing existing information retrieval and natural language processing technologies.

1 Introduction

An intelligent virtual assistant, such as Amazon's Alexa, Microsoft's Cortana, Google Assistant and Apple's Siri, is essentially a voice-based dialog system that provides assistance to users for their daily activities, e.g. making a phone call, checking weather forecast, setting a reminder, and searching for relevant information (Thomas et al., 2017; Burtsev et al., 2017).

Several attempts have been made to develop an intelligent dialog agent using different approaches, including rule-based approaches (e.g. Weizenbaum 1966), machine translation (e.g. Ritter et al. 2011), information retrieval (e.g. Ji et al. 2014), classification

---

The work describes the authors' ideas about the artificial personal shopper task and not of Amazon.

(e.g. Shriberg et al. 1998), sequence-to-sequence models (e.g. Vinyals and Le 2015), reinforcement learning (e.g. Williams and Young 2007) and hybrid approaches (e.g. Bordes et al. 2016). Specifically, in his pioneering work, Weizenbaum (1966) developed the Eliza chatbot agent for interacting with patients with mental illness using syntactic rules. Ritter et al. (2011) learned to respond using phrase-based machine translation from Twitter conversations. Ji et al. (2014) learned to chit-chat from pairs of posts and an associated comments extracted from the Weibo social media platform. Vinyals and Le (2015) created an IT helpdesk dialog system using an encoder-decoder architecture based on recurrent neural networks. Their model converses by predicting the next sentence given the previous sentence or sentences in a conversation. Williams and Young (2007) modeled a dialog conversation as a partially observable Markov decision process (POMDP) and used reinforcement learning to optimize a response action at each time-step by maximizing the cumulative long-term reward.

In this position paper, we introduce a novel artificial personal shopper task, where a voice-based dialog system is used to enrich on-line shopping experience by replicating a personal shopping agent in a brick-and-mortar store. In particular, an effective artificial personal shopper would be able to converse and provide supports for the customer with information related to any products in the on-line store. Importantly, the assistance has to be personalized to individual customers. For example, in order to correctly answer the question "Is the Bose headphone compatible with my phone?", an artificial personal shopper has to know (1) what type of phone the customer has or refers to, (2) what is the model of the 'Bose headphone', and (3) whether *the headphone is compatible with *the customer phone*. Table 1

Proceedings of the 2018 EMNLP Workshop SCAI: The 2nd Int'l Workshop on Search-Oriented Conversational AI, pages 40–45
Brussels, Belgium, October 31, 2018. ©2018 Association for Computational Linguistics

shows some examples of typical shopping related questions associated with potential responses.

The remainder of this paper is organized as follows. In Section 2, we define the artificial personal shopper task and discuss main information types required for handling this task. Section 3 describes some of the research challenges raised by the artificial personal shopper task, and how existing information retrieval (IR) and natural language processing (NLP) approaches could be applied for the task. Section 4 provides concluding remarks.

2 Types of Information Needed for the Personal Shopper Task

In the artificial personal shopper task, an intelligent virtual assistant provides personal shopping services by conducting a meaningful conversation with the customers. To achieve this task, we postulate that the personal assistant should be able to access and leverage three main types of information:

- **Product Information**: Information about the products is crucial for providing useful product-related conversations with the users. An artificial personal shopper should have an efficient and effective access to different forms of information related to each of the products that are available in the e-commerce store in order to answer factual questions about product attributes, functionality, usage, etc. For example, "Can I wear my Fitbit Alta in the shower?" is a typical factual question that can be directly answered based on product information.
- **User Information**: The user information such as previous purchases and browsing history are essential for the artificial personal shopper, as it would enable the inference of the context of the conversation and hence to provide a response that is personalized to individual users. For example, for the question "Is the Bose headphone compatible with my phone?", user information would allow the agent to infer that 'the Bose headphone' is 'a Bose QC35 headphone' by using search or browsing history, and 'my phone' is 'iPhone 6 (with iOS 10.3.2)' according to the purchase history.
- **Customer Generated Content**: Most online stores encourage customers to review and rate products, to submit product-related

questions, and to answer other customer questions. In addition, customers can rate reviews and answers of other customers. This framework of customer generated content (CGC) complements the official information provided by the product provider and enables customers to take better shopping decisions by letting them learn from other customers' experience. Moreover, the CGC data can be used by the artificial shopper assistant for answering subjective questions asking for opinion or advice. For example, the question "Is iPad good for kids?" should be properly responded by extracting information from the iPad related reviews which discuss this particular topic. Typically, different opinions are expected for subjective topics, especially for the controversial ones, hence the agent's response should fairly cover the spectrum of the crowd opinions.

3 Research Challenges

In this section, we introduce research challenges (RCs) regarding how to handle the artificial personal shopper task. In addition, we discuss related work in IR and NLP that could be explored to tackle each of the research challenges.

RC1: How to process a voice utterance?

Advances in automatic speech recognition (ASR), especially with neural networks (e.g. Battenberg et al. 2017), enable an effective automatic transcription from voice to text utterances. Voice interaction opens many opportunity for search-based systems as users tend to provide more detailed questions as well as much more feedback for the search results (Guy, 2016). On the other hand, background noise, cross-talks, different accents, etc., cause many ASR errors. High-accuracy ASR is crucial for this task, as a small error could lead to an incomprehensible or misinterpreted transcribed utterance. Since the ASR technology is not perfect, a robust approach that provides a highly precise response for a noisy utterance is an important research challenge that has to be investigated.

RC2: How to identify relevant response source(s) for a given utterance?

The optimal information sources for response generation should be identified according to the

Utterance	Potential Response
Is my S8 unlocked?	Yes, your Samsung Galaxy S8 is unlocked and can be used with any valid SIM card.
What is the best Kindle to buy?	Kindle PaperWhite is the top high-rated Kindle.
Tell me about Echo Dot.	Echo Dot is a smart speaker developed by Amazon ...
What is the best deal for Instant Pot?	Instant Pot DUO60 is currently 30% off.
Should I buy Galaxy S9 or iPhone 8?	Galaxy S9 has got higher ratings than iPhone 8 ...
Is iPad good for kids?	80% of our customers find that iPad 2017 is not good for kids, while 20% thought it is.
Does Anova Sous Vide make a lot of noise?	95% of our customers say that Anova Sous Vide is very silent in comparison with other products they have.
Is the Bose headphone compatible with my phone?	Bose QC35 headphone cannot be used with your iPhone 6.
I like this pair of Nike shoes.	Good choice. They are the top rating running shoes and match well with the running kit in your shopping cart.

Table 1: Examples of shopping related questions and potential responses from an artificial personal shopper.

utterance characteristics and type. For example, factoid questions should be better answered by the product source while advice questions should be answered by customer generated content. Identifying the proper response sources for a given utterance can be casted as a text categorization task that aims to label a natural language text with a category (or categories) in a pre-defined taxonomy of response sources.

While text categorization (or text classification) has been well-studied in the field of NLP and IR (e.g. Kim et al. 2018; Sebastiani 2002), it would be an interesting research challenge to develop a novel classifier and a set of features that could identify a relevant response source effectively, while minimizing the risk of missing relevant sources for the product domain. Another interesting challenge is how to optimally aggregate the results from different sources. For example, the quality of a question-answer pair can be evaluated according to the support it gets from related customer reviews (McAuley and Yang, 2016).

RC3: How to identify key phrases in a user utterance?

Previous work (e.g. Limsopatham et al. 2014) showed that only a few key terms or key phrases from a natural language query contribute significantly to the quality of the search results. For an artificial personal shopper, these key phrases in the user utterance are mainly the discussed products and their attributes which must be identified in order to support an effective conver-

sation. Many existing techniques can be used to identify key phrases in a given text (e.g. Hulth 2003; Limsopatham and Collier 2016). However, existing key phrase extraction technologies were developed mainly for the general domain, such as websites or newswires, while limited work has been done in the product domain and in the noisy voice transcription domain. For example, an emphasis in the voice signal might be an indicator of a key-phrase. Hence, it is important to investigate into adapting existing approaches, and developing new domain specific approaches, to effectively extract key phrases from utterances for the artificial personal shopper task.

RC4: How to infer which product/entity the user refers to?

Another challenge of an artificial personal shopper is to infer which product or entity the user refers to. This is different from the traditional entity resolution task (e.g. Leidner et al. 2003) that mainly identify or match relevant entities in a pre-define ontology within the text. In the setting of an artificial personal shopper the entity resolution task is more complex since personalized information must be taken into consideration. For example, as already has been shown in Section 2, for the question "Is the Bose headphone compatible with my phone?", the system needs to infer that 'Bose headphone' is 'a Bose QC35 headphone' and 'my phone' is 'iPhone 6 (with iOS 10.3.2)', by using information from different sources, including browsing history, purchase history, and the question itself. This would be an interesting area of research that needs to incorporate co-reference resolution and anaphora resolution for grounding personal shopper products/entities.

RC5: How to generate a natural language response?

Assuming that we could retrieve a piece of information that is relevant to the user utterance, the next major challenge is to generate a friendly conversational response that contains the relevant information as part of the continues dialog. Such a response should be comprehensive and complete while still concise and short. Several approaches could be investigated and extended for the task, including snippet generation (Turpin et al., 2007), text summarization (Spärck Jones, 2007) and natural language text generation (Wen et al., 2015). Nevertheless, a response from a snippet generation technique (Turpin et al., 2007) may be informational but non-conversational, while on the other hand, a response from a language generation technique (Wen et al., 2015) would be conversational but may not answer properly the user question. Therefore, an effective approach for generating informative and conversational responses is an interesting and open research challenge.

Another interesting aspect of this challenge is generating a multi-facet answer to a subjective question that represents the crowd's multi opinions respectfully and truthfully. In contrast to factoid questions, subjective questions can have many valid answers since there is no absolute ground truth. A multi-aspect answer shall cover the distribution of the crowd opinions over the answer aspect space. The final answer should represent the selected aspects with their accumulated sentiment as reflected in the CGC data.

RC6: How to evaluate an end-to-end personal shopper system?

The evaluation of conversational agents is a research area that has not attracted much attention by the research community. Goh et al. (2007) discusses the inappropriateness of existing IR measures for response quality evaluation, and calls for new standard measures and related considerations. Radziwill and Benton (2017) presents a literature review of quality issues with chatbots. Most evaluation approaches rely on having human evaluators provide their subjective views of the system's performance.

Another possible evaluation paradigm is based on n-gram similarities, such as BLEU (Papineni et al., 2002) and ROUGE (Lin, 2004), which are typically used for machine translation and text summarization tasks. Within this paradigm, a dialog system is evaluated based on the overlap between an n-gram set of its response and that of the ground truth (Papineni et al., 2002; Lin, 2004).

In contrast, question-answering evaluation has been studied extensively (Voorhees and Tice, 2000; Rajpurkar et al., 2016). However, these studies mainly focused on factoid questions. The TREC's LiveQA track (Agichtein et al., 2015) evaluated the ability of a QA system to answer complex Yahoo Answers questions in real time. Human editors judged the answer quality. In general, automatic answers quality was far from being satisfiable, compared to human answers.

Nevertheless, responses from an artificial personal shopper have to be conversational. Therefore, how to evaluate the responses based on the criteria of both the relevance toward the user's information needs and the replication of a human-like conversation would be an interesting research challenge.

4 Conclusions

We have introduced the personal shopper task for an intelligent virtual assistant, where the goal is to develop novel technologies to aid on-line voice shopping. In particular, we highlighted challenges of developing such a system and discussed how existing IR and NLP techniques could be adapted and extended to deal with challenges of the task. Achieving this task would pave a way for intelligent virtual assistants to perform more complex tasks in conversational search, and stimulate further research.

References

Eugene Agichtein, David Carmel, Dan Pelleg, Yuval Pinter, and Donna Harman. 2015. Overview of the trec 2015 liveqa track. In *TREC*.

Eric Battenberg, Jitong Chen, Rewon Child, Adam Coates, Yashesh Gaur Yi Li, Hairong Liu, Sanjeev Satheesh, Anuroop Sriram, and Zhenyao Zhu. 2017. Exploring neural transducers for end-to-end speech recognition. In *Automatic Speech Recognition and Understanding Workshop (ASRU), 2017 IEEE*, pages 206–213. IEEE.

Antoine Bordes, Y-Lan Boureau, and Jason Weston. 2016. Learning end-to-end goal-oriented dialog. *arXiv preprint arXiv:1605.07683*.

Mikhail Burtsev, Aleksandr Chuklin, Julia Kiseleva, and Alexey Borisov. 2017. Search-oriented conversational ai (scai). In *Proceedings of the ACM SIGIR International Conference on Theory of Information Retrieval*, ICTIR '17, pages 333–334, New York, NY, USA. ACM.

Ong Sing Goh, C. Ardil, W. Wong, and C.C. Fung. 2007. A black-box approach for response quality evaluation of conversational agent systems. *International Journal of Computational Intelligence*, pages 195–203.

Ido Guy. 2016. Searching by talking: Analysis of voice queries on mobile web search. In *Proceedings of the 39th International ACM SIGIR Conference on Research and Development in Information Retrieval*, SIGIR '16, pages 35–44, New York, NY, USA. ACM.

Anette Hulth. 2003. Improved automatic keyword extraction given more linguistic knowledge. In *Proceedings of the 2003 Conference on Empirical Methods in Natural Language Processing*, EMNLP '03, pages 216–223, Stroudsburg, PA, USA. Association for Computational Linguistics.

Zongcheng Ji, Zhengdong Lu, and Hang Li. 2014. An information retrieval approach to short text conversation. *arXiv preprint arXiv:1408.6988*.

Young-Bum Kim, Dongchan Kim, Joo-Kyung Kim, and Ruhi Sarikaya. 2018. A scalable neural shortlisting-reranking approach for large-scale domain classification in natural language understanding. In *Proceedings of the 2018 Conference of the North American Chapter of the Association for Computational Linguistics: Human Language Technologies, Volume 3 (Industry Papers)*, volume 3, pages 16–24.

Jochen L Leidner, Gail Sinclair, and Bonnie Webber. 2003. Grounding spatial named entities for information extraction and question answering. In *Proceedings of the HLT-NAACL 2003 workshop on Analysis of geographic references-Volume 1*, pages 31–38.

Nut Limsopatham and Nigel Collier. 2016. Bidirectional lstm for named entity recognition in twitter messages. In *Proceedings of the 2nd Workshop on Noisy User-generated Text (WNUT)*, pages 145–152.

Nut Limsopatham, Craig Macdonald, and Iadh Ounis. 2014. Modelling relevance towards multiple inclusion criteria when ranking patients. In *Proceedings of the 23rd ACM International Conference on Conference on Information and Knowledge Management*, pages 1639–1648. ACM.

Chin-Yew Lin. 2004. Rouge: A package for automatic evaluation of summaries. *Text Summarization Branches Out*.

Julian McAuley and Alex Yang. 2016. Addressing complex and subjective product-related queries with customer reviews. In *Proceedings of the 25th International Conference on World Wide Web*, WWW '16, pages 625–635, Republic and Canton of Geneva, Switzerland. International World Wide Web Conferences Steering Committee.

Kishore Papineni, Salim Roukos, Todd Ward, and Wei-Jing Zhu. 2002. Bleu: a method for automatic evaluation of machine translation. In *Proceedings of the 40th annual meeting on association for computational linguistics*, pages 311–318. Association for Computational Linguistics.

Nicole M. Radziwill and Morgan C. Benton. 2017. Evaluating quality of chatbots and intelligent conversational agents. *CoRR*, abs/1704.04579.

Pranav Rajpurkar, Jian Zhang, Konstantin Lopyrev, and Percy Liang. 2016. Squad: 100,000+ questions for machine comprehension of text. *arXiv preprint arXiv:1606.05250*.

Alan Ritter, Colin Cherry, and William B Dolan. 2011. Data-driven response generation in social media. In *Proceedings of the conference on empirical methods in natural language processing*, pages 583–593.

Fabrizio Sebastiani. 2002. Machine learning in automated text categorization. *ACM computing surveys (CSUR)*, 34(1):1–47.

Elizabeth Shriberg, Andreas Stolcke, Daniel Jurafsky, Noah Coccaro, Marie Meteer, Rebecca Bates, Paul Taylor, Klaus Ries, Rachel Martin, and Carol Van Ess-Dykema. 1998. Can prosody aid the automatic classification of dialog acts in conversational speech? *Language and speech*, 41(3-4):443–492.

Karen Spärck Jones. 2007. Automatic summarising: The state of the art. *Inf. Process. Manage.*, 43(6):1449–1481.

Paul Thomas, Daniel McDuff, Mary Czerwinski, and Nick Craswell. 2017. Misc: A data set of information-seeking conversations. In *SIGIR 1st International Workshop on Conversational Approaches to Information Retrieval (CAIR'17)*, volume 5.

Andrew Turpin, Yohannes Tsegay, David Hawking, and Hugh E Williams. 2007. Fast generation of result snippets in web search. In *Proceedings of the 30th annual international ACM SIGIR conference on Research and development in information retrieval*, pages 127–134. ACM.

Oriol Vinyals and Quoc Le. 2015. A neural conversational model. *arXiv preprint arXiv:1506.05869*.

Ellen M. Voorhees and Dawn M. Tice. 2000. Building a question answering test collection. In *Proceedings of the 23rd Annual International ACM SIGIR Conference on Research and Development in Information Retrieval*, SIGIR '00, pages 200–207, New York, NY, USA. ACM.

Joseph Weizenbaum. 1966. Eliza a computer program for the study of natural language communication between man and machine. *Communications of the ACM*, 9(1):36–45.

Tsung-Hsien Wen, Milica Gasic, Nikola Mrkšić, Pei-Hao Su, David Vandyke, and Steve Young. 2015. Semantically conditioned lstm-based natural language generation for spoken dialogue systems. In *Proceedings of the 2015 Conference on Empirical Methods in Natural Language Processing*, pages 1711–1721.

Jason D Williams and Steve Young. 2007. Partially observable markov decision processes for spoken dialog systems. *Computer Speech & Language*, 21(2):393–422.

Curriculum Learning Based on Reward Sparseness for Deep Reinforcement Learning of Task Completion Dialogue Management

Atsushi Saito

Nextremer Co., Ltd., Tokyo, Japan.

`atsushi.saito@nextremer.com`

Abstract

Learning from sparse and delayed reward is a central issue in reinforcement learning. In this paper, to tackle reward sparseness problem of task oriented dialogue management, we propose a curriculum based approach on the number of slots of user goals. This curriculum makes it possible to learn dialogue management for sets of user goals with large number of slots. We also propose a dialogue policy based on progressive neural networks whose modules with parameters are appended with previous parameters fixed as the curriculum proceeds, and this policy improves performances over the one with single set of parameters.

1 Introduction

Learning in environments that give agents sparse and delayed reward is still a central research issue in reinforcement learning, while there are remarkable successes of deep reinforcement learning methods(Mnih et al., 2016; Bellemare et al., 2016; Ostrovski et al., 2017; Vezhnevets et al., 2017; Riedmiller et al., 2018).

The problem on sparse and delayed reward appears in reinforcement learning for task oriented dialogue agents. Contrary to single turn interactions such as chit-chat or question answering (Serban et al., 2016; Li et al., 2016), task oriented dialogue agents often are required to retrieve information from external knowledge bases and to learn the way how the agent reasons with progression of dialogue tasks over multiple dialog turns(Young et al., 2013; Williams et al., 2017). This long term process, however, makes it difficult for Markov Decision Process to identify the part of an action sequence that affects progress of dialogue tasks over multiple turns. Thus, typical agents must decide from a positive reward, which is obtained from successful task completion, only at the last turn.

It is inevitable for practical scalability to use sparse reward functions, because designing complicated and dense reward criteria over multiple turns involves domain knowledge and human annotators to evaluate dialogue history of large size. In particular, our aim is to train dialogue policy agents that cannot obtain positive rewards until the last turn.

While general and scalable frameworks of task completion dialogue management have been proposed recently, these frameworks still have had reward sparseness problem. Li et al. (2017) proposed a general neural dialogue framework which has scalability and features to solve information retrieval tasks (TC-Bot), which extended a previous work on information retrieval dialogue system (called KB-Info-Bot) to access external knowledge base (Dhingra et al., 2017). While they firstly proposed a robust end-to-end modularized neural dialogue system with separated and independently trainable modules, which are natural language understanding, dialogue management, and natural language generation, difficulty in reinforcement learning with sparse rewards still remains for their learning method with deep Q-networks (DQN).

In this paper, we propose curriculum learning based on reward sparseness of user goals, and agents using progressive neural networks (Rusu et al., 2016a) to improve the curriculum learning.

Our contribution is two-fold. First, our curriculum learning makes it possible to learn sets of user goals with large number of slots for which TC-Bot failed to learn. As the simulation epoch increases, the minimum number of slots that user goals contain increases.(See an overview in Figure 1) For example, the minimum number of slots is two for the first 200 simulation epochs, and is four for the next 200 ones, and agents are finally

Proceedings of the 2018 EMNLP Workshop SCAI: The 2nd Int'l Workshop on Search-Oriented Conversational AI, pages 46–51
Brussels, Belgium, October 31, 2018. ©2018 Association for Computational Linguistics

trained with user goals that contains at least 10 slots. In other words, the more simulation epoch proceeds, the more sparse reward is obtained from environments. There are two practical advantages of this curriculum: (1) our curriculum is domain free and (2) curriculum data preparation is easy because our curriculum only depends on the number of slots of user goals.

Second, the proposed application of progressive neural networks improves knowledge transfer from models trained for easier curriculum data to models trained for harder one. Progressive neural networks have multiple columns with weight parameters. At first a progressive neural network has single column to be trained, then another column is appended with new parameter set. All parameters of previous columns are frozen when appended column is training, and the appended columns can exploit information from frozen columns. Our aim is to apply this progressive freezing mechanism to exploit information of the parameters that are trained with *easier user goals* of our curriculum, when the latest appended column is in training with *harder user goals*. This progressive exploitation is expected to overcome the difficulty in the setting that agents start reinforcement learning with *the hardest user goals*.

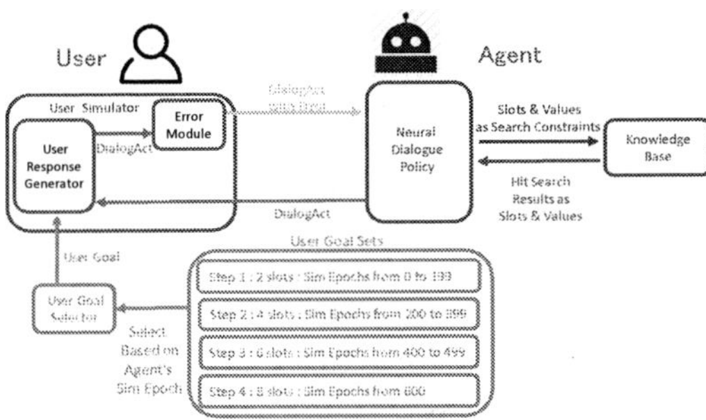

Figure 1: Overview of the way how to switch user goals.

2   Related Work

Task Oriented Dialogue   One of the most popular models to learn task oriented (or goal oriented) dialogue is Partially Observable Markov Decision Process(POMDP) (Young et al., 2013; Verena Rieser,, 2010; Gasic et al., 2013). Another line of research is end-to-end neural modeling (Serban et al., 2016; Williams and Zweig, 2016; Liu and Lane, 2017a,b; Liu et al., 2018). While methods based on supervised learning are proposed in (Bordes et al., 2017; Wen et al., 2017), they come with the uncertainty of model performance for unknown data of interactions with humans. (Dhingra et al., 2017) proposed Reinforcement Learning dialog agent for learning the way how to access information of external knowledge base.

Progressive Neural Networks   Originally, the notion of progressive neural networks is proposed in the research to transfer learning across multiple tasks and foreknowledge task similarity (Rusu et al., 2016a). Comparing with the original use of progressive neural networks, in our application, each column is *not necessary to be trained until convergence*, that is, our purpose is to provide the last column supplemental information, which is transfered from parameter weights obtained in environments with more dense reward. An application in robotic manipulations show, the way to adopt models that are trained in 3D simulation environments to real world physical environments (Rusu et al., 2016b). Similar to the approach of this paper, they tried to avoid designing complicated reward functions for application settings in real world.

Curriculum Learning   The first proposition of the concept of curriculum learning is in (Bengio et al., 2009). While their curriculum data sets are based on complexity of shapes and graduation of colors to train image recognition models and the vocabulary size to train language models, our proposed curriculum data is based on the number of slots of user goals to solve goal oriented dialogue tasks and yields a kind of sub tasks that we can regard filling one slot as a sub task of filling two or more slots. The curriculum data set used in our experiment was created from slot types and their values of the movie search data set in (Li et al., 2017). The proposed method trains progressive neural networks to transfer knowledge across sets of user goals, and a theoretical relationship between transfer learning and curriculum learning is studied in (Weinshall et al., 2018).

3   Reinforcement Learning for Task Completion Dialogue Management

Task Completion Dialogue

Task completion dialogue management contains the following elements: user goals, task completed status, user simulators. These elements constitute reinforcement learning environments. More specific descriptions are as follows.

User goals: User goals contain two kinds of information : (1) pairs of slots and the values that users want to inform to systems as a constraint of items to be retrieved from knowledge base and (2) slots whose values are unknown for agents but they want to obtain the values of these slots.

Definition of task completed status: The dialogues between agents and users is defined as successful, if only if agents have proposed the slots and values based on retrieved information from knowledge base such that the following two conditions are satisfied: (1) these slots and values satisfy the constraints of user goals and (2) proposed slot types are requested in user goals.

User simulators: User simulators send a dialogue act, which provides a representation of the hidden semantics of a user utterance. There are two kinds of dialogue acts: (1) ones depending on slot types act like *inform* or *request* whose example is represented as a pair $(inform, movie\ name)$ and (2) ones independent of them such as *greeting* or *completing the task* etc.

Reinforcement Learning Agents and Environments

In here, we provide an explanation on actions of agents and state representations and reward functions which constitute Markov reward models of task completion dialogue management.

Agents' actions: Actions of reinforcement learning agents are dialogue acts and each dialogue act has at most one slot. The number of actions, which is also the dimensionality of action vectors, is the sum of the following: the number of inform slots, the number of request slots, and the number of actions that are independent on slot types.

State representations: State representations that agents can observe contain multiple kinds of vectors. These vectors include binary vectors representing subsets of inform slots or request slots, and include one-hot vectors representing current turn number. These vectors are necessary for agents to recognize progress of dialogue tasks. The state representation also contains information from external knowledge base such as lists of items in knowledge base that satisfy the users' requests and the sizes of these lists. State representations at time t also contain one-hot vectors of the agent's action at time $t - 1$.

Reward functions: A large positive reward $2T_{max}$ is given to agents if dialogue status have been successful, and a negative reward $-2T_{max}$ is given for the failed status, where T_{max} is the maximum number of dialogue turns. We note that each of agent and user can send an utterance at most a half of T_{max} times. Additionally, for each turn, the negative reward -1 is given to the agents.

Finally, we describe the way to update deep Q-networks and a note on initialization of experience replay memory (ERM). Updates of Q-networks are performed with Bellman Equation and Mean Squared Error(MSE). An experience replay memory stores the transitions of agents. During initial experience, to avoid the cold start problem, agents use rule based policy, which essentially request each slot type, and stores the transitions obtained by this rule based policy. Then, agents start the training phase of deep Q-learning. Once DQN agent's performance on success rate overtakes rule based policy, ERM is set to an empty list.

4 Proposed Methods

Curriculum of User Goals

In here, we describe our curriculum of user goals. The purpose of this curriculum is to investigate the performance of dialogue management for the set in which *only user goals with large number of slots* are contained. Four sets of user goals were prepared. The minimum number of slots for each user goal set is showed in Table 1.

Set	inf	req	all
A	1	1	2
B	2	2	4
C	3	3	6
D	6	2	8

Table 1: The minimum number of slots for each user goal set. The three labels **inf, req, all** respectively correspond to the number of inform slots, request slots, and all slots.

Step	Range	User Goal Set
1	0-199	$A \cup B \cup C \cup D$
2	200-399	$B \cup C \cup D$
3	400-599	$C \cup D$
4	600-1200	D

Table 2: Set of user goals selected in each simulation epoch range of our curriculum. The sets A,B,C,and D are defined in Table 1

The pairs of the ranges of simulation epochs and the corresponding set of user goals are showed in

	slot type	value
inform slots	city	Seattle
request slots	theater	Unknown

Table 3: An example of easy user goals in Step 1. Users can obtain one of many names of theaters in Seattle.

	slot type	value
inform slots	starttime	19:00
	genre	history
	date	August 31
	actor	Tom Hanks
	city	Seattle
request slots	theater	Unknown
	moviename	Unknown

Table 4: An example of hard user goals in Step 4. Users can obtain a name of movie **The post** and a name of theater **Admiral Theater** for *moviename* slot and *theater* slot, respectively.

Table 2. We consider the difficulty of sets of user goals as follows: the less slots a set of user goals contains, the easier the set of user goals is. In our curriculum, at first, a user goal is randomly sampled from the union of all sets of user goals defined in Table 1. Then, as the step proceeds to the next one, the easiest set of user goals is removed from the union.Thus, at last, the set D which contains only hardest user goals is used for simulation. Examples of user goals are showed in Table 3 and Table 4.

We note that our curriculum training method takes into account the possibly varying order of slots during training, because agents must fill all slots which users have informed with an arbitrary order in our experiments.

There are two remarks of our curriculum. First, the longest dialog episodes with no redundant agent's action are yielded from the set D. That is, the proposed training process does not concatenate dialogs from different sets as training goes on. Second, each of four sets of user goals in Table 1 has a variety of types of slots, because each set of user goals was created by choosing random pairs of slot type and its value.

Thus, the proposed curriculum can be created from all kinds of data sets of user goals for task completion dialogue based on slot filling, and the proposed training process does not depend on data sets of user goals.

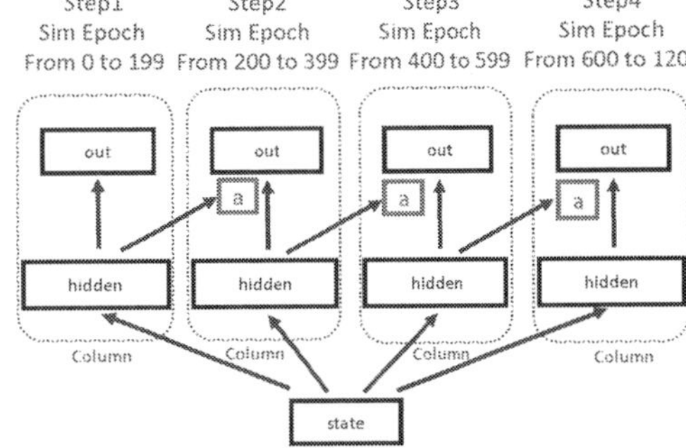

Figure 2: Training Process via Progressive Nets: As the curriculum step increases, new columns are appended. Green modules represent adaptors.

Progressive Neural Dialogue Policy

In here, we describe the notion of progressive neural networks and its applications to our setting (See Figure 2 for an overview). We define feature vectors of frozen columns as $h_{i-1}^{(<k)} = [h_{i-1}^{(1)}; h_{i-1}^{(2)}; ...; h_{i-1}^{(k-1)}]$ of dimensionality $n_{i-1}^{(<k)}$, where the symbol ; denotes concatenating. Progressive networks have lateral connections through which we leverage prior knowledge to previously learned features and they have their own activation functions. Before feeding the lateral activations into linear layer, we multiply them by a trainable scalar called scaling factor, initialized by a random small value to adopt for the different scales of the different inputs. The hidden layer of the non-linear adapter is a projection onto an n_i dimensional subspace. We denote $W_i^{(k)} \in \mathbb{R}^{n_i \times n_{i-1}}$ as the weight matrix of layer i of column k, and denote $U^{(k:j)} \in \mathbb{R}^{n_i \times n_{i-1}}$ as the lateral connections from layer $i - 1$ of column j, to layer i of column k and h_0 is the network input. Thus, the output of the i-th layer of k-th column is:

$$h_i^{(k)} = \sigma(W_i^{(k)} h_{i-1}^{(k)} + U_i^{(k:j)} \sigma(V_i^{(k:j)} \alpha_{i-1}^{(<k)} h_{i-1}^{(k)}))$$

, where $V_i^{(k:j)}$ is the projection matrix and $\alpha_{i-1}^{(<k)}$ is the scaling factor, σ is ReLU function, and bias terms are omitted. In our curriculum learning, an agent has a deep Q-network represented as a progressive neural network, and new column is appended when the step in Table 2 is count up. In our settings, the number of hidden layers is one, and its size of units is 80.

5   Experiments

Reinforcement Learning Environments and Data Set The curriculum data of user goals for the experiments was created from the movie searching data set used in (Li et al., 2017). The same reinforcement learning environment and user simulator in (Li et al., 2017) was used for the experiments.

User Simulator In our experiments, user simulators try to let dialogue agents fill slots which users have informed. The simulators also inform values of slots which users have requested as constraints to retrieve values from a data base. If the simulators have a slot type which they have not informed yet, they also inform its value. The simulators inform the value *I don't care* if agents have requested values of a slot type which is not contained in inform slots of user goals. For example, the simulators with the user goal showed in Table 4 send the message *I don't care*, when agents have requested the value of slot type *price*, because *price* slot type is not contained in inform slots in Table 4.

Setup of Experiments RMSprop was used as the optimizer. The hyper parameters of the optimizer were set to the following values: the learning rate, the decay rate and the momentum were, 0.001, 0.999, and 0.1, respectively. With the way similar to (Li et al., 2017), the error control model that has two kinds of errors: slot level and intent level was used. In the experiment, slot level and intent level correspond to the case where the slot name is correctly recognized but the slot value is wrong and the case where a dialogue act itself is wrongfully recognized, respectively. For each simulation epoch there are 100 episodes of dialogue between users and agents. In each episode of dialogue, a user can send an utterance at most a half of T_{max} times and an agent can perform in the same way.

Results The success rate (moving average with window of size 7) of each simulation epoch is shown in Figure 3. This figure shows that progressive neural network can make learning faster, noting that agents were trained for the set D in Table 1 for simulation epoch more than 600. The simulation in which agents are trained with only the user goal set D for all simulation epochs was also executed. The success rates for this hardest simulation were 0.0 for all simulation epochs and for all of six error settings (omitted in Figure 3). In particular, for the success rates in 3b and 3c, pro-

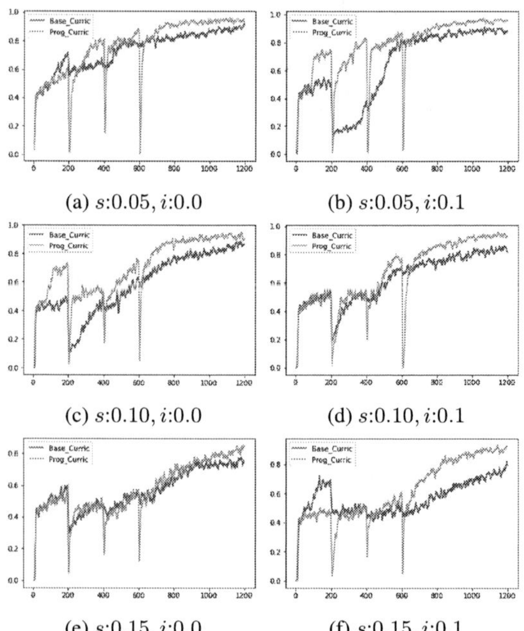

(a) s:0.05, i:0.0　　　(b) s:0.05, i:0.1

(c) s:0.10, i:0.0　　　(d) s:0.10, i:0.1

(e) s:0.15, i:0.0　　　(f) s:0.15, i:0.1

Figure 3: For slot level error ϵ and intent level error δ, the caption of each figure is written as s:ϵ,i:δ. Blue lines correspond to curriculum learning deep-Q-networks, and Orange lines correspond to progressive neural network models.

gressive neural networks improve the performance for all simulation epoch ranges in Table 2, while the success rates for progressive networks drop at switching epochs(200, 400, 600).

6   Conclusion

In this paper, we introduce a curriculum on reward sparseness of user goals to tackle reward sparseness problem in reinforcement learning for task completion dialogue management, and this curriculum makes it possible to learn via reinforcement learning of dialogue management task using user goals with large number of slots. We also propose a method based on progressive neural networks to improve learning performance. Experiments show that progressive neural networks enhance the curriculum reinforcement learning.

Acknowledgements

The author wishes to thank Taichi Iki, Yuki Sekizawa, and the anonymous reviewers for helpful comments.

References

Marc G. Bellemare, Sriram Srinivasan, Georg Ostrovski, Tom Schaul, David Saxton, and Remi Munos. 2016. Unifying count-based exploration and intrinsic motivation. In *NIPS2016*.

Yoshua Bengio, Jerome Louradour, Ronan Collober, and Jason Weston. 2009. Curriculum learning. In *ICML2009*.

Antoine Bordes, Y-Lan Boureau, and Jason Weston. 2017. Learning end-to-end goal-oriented dialog. In *ICLR2017*.

Bhuwan Dhingra, Lihong Li, Xiujun Li, Jianfeng Gao, Yun-Nung Chen, Faisal Ahmed, and Li Deng. 2017. Towards end-to-end reinforcement learning of dialogue agents for information access. In *ACL2017*. pages 484 – 495.

Milica Gasic, Catherine Breslin, Matthew Henderson, Dongho Kim, Martin Szummer, Blaise Thomson, Pirros Tsiakoulis, and Steve Young. 2013. Online policy optimisation of bayesian spoken dialogue systems via human interaction. In *IEEE ICASSP*. pages 8367–8371.

Jiwei Li, Michel Galley, Chris Brockett, Georgios P Spithourakis, Jianfeng Gao, and Bill Dolan. 2016. A persona-based neural conversation model. In *ACL2016*.

Xiujun Li, Yun-Nung Chen, Lihong Li, Jianfeng Gao, and Asli Celikyilmaz. 2017. End-to-end task-completion neural dialogue systems. In *IJCNLP2017*.

Bing Liu and Ian Lane. 2017a. An end-to-end trainable neural network model with belief tracking for task-oriented dialog. *arXiv:1708.05956* .

Bing Liu and Ian Lane. 2017b. Iterative policy learning in end-to-end trainable task-oriented neural dialog models. In *IEEE Workshop on Automatic Speech Recognition and Understanding(ASRU)*.

Bing Liu, Gokhan Tur, Dilek Hakkani-Tur, Pararth Shah, and Larry Heck. 2018. Dialogue learning with human teaching and feedback in end-to-end trainable task-oriented dialogue systems. In *NAACL2018*.

Volodymyr Mnih, Koray Kavukcuoglu, David Silver, Andrei A. Rusu, Joel Veness, Marc G. Bellemare, Alex Graves, Martin Riedmiller, Andreas K. Fidjeland, Georg Ostrovski, Stig Petersen, Charles Beattie, Amir Sadik, Ioannis Antonoglou, Helen King, Dharshan Kumaran, Daan Wierstra, Shane Legg, and Demis Hassabis. 2016. Human-level control through deep reinforcement learning. *Nature* 518:529–533.

Georg Ostrovski, Marc G. Bellemare, Aaron van den Oord, and Remi Munos. 2017. Count-based exploration with neural density models. In *ICML2017*.

Martin Riedmiller, Roland Hafner, Thomas Lampe, Michael Neunert, Jonas Degrave, Tom Van de Wiele, Volodymyr Mnih, Nicolas Heess, and Jost Tobias Springenberg. 2018. Learning by playing - solving sparse reward tasks from scratch. *arXiv:1802.10567* .

Andrei A. Rusu, Neil C. Rabinowitz, Guillaume Desjardins, Hubert Soyer, James Kirkpatrick, Koray Kavukcuoglu, Razvan Pascanu, and Raia Hadsell. 2016a. Progressive neural networks. *arXiv:1606.04671* .

Andrei A. Rusu, Mel Vecerik, Thomas Rothrl, Nicolas Heess, Razvan Pascanu, and Raia Hadsell. 2016b. Sim-to-real robot learning from pixels with progressive nets. *arXiv:1610.04286* .

Iulian V Serban, Alessandro Sordoni, Yoshua Bengio, Aaron Courville, and Joelle Pineau. 2016. Building end-to-end dialogue systems using generative hierarchical neural network models. In *AAAI2016*.

Oliver Lemon Verena Rieser,. 2010. *Reinforcement Learning for Adaptive Dialogue Systems*. Springer. In chapter 2, section 2.1, page 10.

Alexander Sasha Vezhnevets, Simon Osindero, Tom Schaul, Nicolas Heess, Max Jaderberg, David Silver, and Koray Kavukcuoglu. 2017. Feudal networks for hierarchical reinforcement learning. *arXiv:1703.01161* .

Daphna Weinshall, Gad Cohen, and Dan Amir. 2018. Curriculum learning by transfer learning: Theory and experiments with deep networks. *arXiv:1802.03796* .

Tsung-Hsien Wen, David Vandyke, Nikola Mrksic, Milica Gasic, Lina M. Rojas-Barahona, Pei-Hao Su, Stefan Ultes, and Steve Young. 2017. A network based end-to-end trainable task-oriented dialogue system. In *EACL2017*.

Jason D Williams, Kavosh Asadi, and Geoffrey Zweig. 2017. Hybrid code networks: practical and efficient end-to-end dialog control with supervised and reinforcement learning. In *ACL2017*.

Jason D. Williams and Geoffrey Zweig. 2016. End-to-end lstm-based dialog control optimized with supervised and reinforcement learning. *arXiv:1606.01269* .

Steve Young, Milica Gasic, Blaise Thomson, and Jason D Williams. 2013. Pomdp-based statistical spoken dialog systems: A review. *IEEE* 101(5):1160 – 1179.

Data Augmentation for Neural Online Chat Response Selection

Wenchao Du
Language Technology Institute
Carnegie Mellon University
Pittsburgh, PA 15213
wenchaod@cs.cmu.edu

Alan W Black
Language Technology Institute
Carnegie Mellon University
Pittsburgh, PA 15213
awb@cs.cmu.edu

Abstract

Data augmentation seeks to manipulate the available data for training to improve the generalization ability of models. We investigate two data augmentation proxies, permutation and flipping, for neural dialog response selection task on various models over multiple datasets, including both Chinese and English languages. Different from standard data augmentation techniques, our method combines the original and synthesized data for prediction. Empirical results show that our approach can gain 1 to 3 recall-at-1 points over baseline models in both full-scale and small-scale settings.

1 Introduction

Building machines that are capable of conversing like humans is one of the primary goals of artificial intelligence. Extensive manual labor is typically required by traditional rule-based systems, limiting the scalability of such systems across multiple domains. With the success of machine learning, the quest of building data-driven dialog systems has come into focus over the past few years (Ritter et al., 2011). Existing approaches in this area can be categorized into generation-based methods and retrieval-based methods. While generation-based methods are still far from reliably generating informative responses, retrieval-based methods have the advantage of fluency and groundedness, since they select responses from existing data. We concentrate on retrieval-based methods in this paper, though we believe the proposed techniques could also improve generation-based models.

While current state-of-the-art results for dialog models are achieved by deep learning approaches, the performance of neural models largely depends on the amount of training data. However, acquiring conversational data can be difficult at times. On the other hand, even with thousands of data points, it is unclear whether these models can optimally benefit from them. Therefore, data augmentation and its efficient use becomes an important problem. Our main contribution is that we investigated new ways to manipulate chat data and neural model architectures to improve performance. To our knowledge, we are the first to evaluate data augmentation on different types of neural conversation models over multiple domains and languages.

2 Data Augmentation

Recent studies (Adi et al., 2016; Khandelwal et al., 2018) have shown that recurrent neural networks (RNN), especially long-short term memory networks (LSTM), are sensitive to word order when encoding contextual information. However, for the response selection task, it is so far unclear to what extent word order is important. This problem is perplexed by the following language phenomena we observed from existing chat data:

1. Broken continuity. Simultaneous conversations happen in multi-party dialogs (Elsner and Charniak, 2008) very often, resulting in some utterances not responding to their immediately preceding ones. Even in conversations between only two people, continuity may still break due to one person switch topic before the other responds. See Table 1 for examples.

2. Mixed turn-taking behavior. People can give multiple utterances before the other respond. Usually, these consecutive messages from same person form arguments that are in parallel (by 'argument' we mean text spans that form discourse relations with each other), and their orderings are not that important. We found this to be very common in online live chats. See Table 2 for examples.

Proceedings of the 2018 EMNLP Workshop SCAI: The 2nd Int'l Workshop on Search-Oriented Conversational AI, pages 52–58
Brussels, Belgium, October 31, 2018. ©2018 Association for Computational Linguistics

Example 1:

Old	I dont run graphical ubuntu, I run ubuntu server.
Kuja	Haha sucker.
Taru	?
Burner	you can use "ps ax" and "kill (PID#)"
Kuja	Anyways, you made the changes right?

Example 2:

Customer	在(there) 吗(?)
Customer	看看(look at) 此(this) 款(one)
Agent	在的(I'm here) 亲(dear)
Agent	亲(dear)，请(please) 发(send) 链接(link)

Table 1: Example chat snippets for broken continuity. The first example is from (Lowe et al., 2015). Burner's message is responding to Old, and Kuja's last message is replying to Taru. The second example is from Taobao, where the third message is responding to the first message, and the fourth message to the second message.

Example 1:

Customer A	这(this) 款(one) 我(I) 穿(wear) 什么(what) 码(size)
Customer A	160高(tall)，107 斤(0.5kg) 重(heavy)
Agent	亲(dear) 如果(if) 喜欢(like) 宽松(loose) 点的就(then) 可以(can) 选(choose) L 哦

Example 2:

Customer B	158cm
Customer B	63kg
Customer B	穿(wear) 什么(what) 码(size) 的合适(fit)
Agent	亲(dear) 根据(based on) 亲的(your) 数据(data)，建议(suggest) 穿(wear) L 码(size)

Table 2: Example chat snippets for mixed turn-taking from Taobao. The question for recommendation and its relevant information (height and weight) can be communicated through different number of utterances in arbitrary order.

Example:

Wizard	Sorry, I cannot find any trips leaving from Gotham City. Could you suggest another nearby departure city?
Customer	Would any packages to Mos Eisley be available, if I increase my budget to $2500?
Wizard	There are no trips available to Mos Eisley.

Table 3: Example chat snippets from Frames. The first message has two sentences. The second message is a conditional complex sentence.

Example 2 of Table 1 after Permutation:

Customer	在(there) 吗(?)
Agent	在的(I'm here) 亲(dear)
Customer	看看(look at) 此(this) 款(one)
Agent	亲(dear)，请(please) 发(send) 链接(link)

Example 1 of Table 2 after Permutation:

Customer A	160高(tall)，107 斤(0.5kg) 重(heavy)
Customer A	这(this) 款(one) 我(I) 穿(wear) 什么(what) 码(size)
Agent	亲(dear) 如果(if) 喜欢(like) 宽松(loose) 点的就(then) 可以(can) 选(choose) L 哦

Example of Table 3 after Flipping:

Wizard	Could you suggest another nearby departure city? Sorry, I cannot find any trips leaving from Gotham City.
Customer	if I increase my budget to $2500, Would any packages to Mos Eisley be available?
Wizard	There are no trips available to Mos Eisley.

Table 4: Results of proposed transformations on previous examples. In the first and second examples, the two messages right before the last agent's response are permuted. In the third example, the first message is flipped, splitting at the period; the second messages is separated at the comma and flipped.

3. Long utterances. Some utterances contain multiple sentences. Some are single compound sentence with multiple clauses. See Table 3 for examples.

To summarize, the critical information for responding, which can be either a single word, phrase, or a full sentence, may have varying relative positions in the context. Therefore, we hypothesize that there exist alternative orderings of utterances and intra-utterance arguments in chat data that can help selecting responses, given recurrent neural models' sensitivity to word order. In this paper, our main goal is to seek improvement by creating variations in the ordering of utterances and arguments. We aim for *generic* methods, bypassing the need of discourse and syntactic parsing as an intermediate step. With the fact that online chats are typically noisy with spelling errors and ungrammaticality, a relative lack of precision may actually help. We therefore propose the following ways to manipulate chat data:

Permutation is simply reversing the order of any two messages in the context. This may help recover the continuity or create alternative ordering of parallel arguments.

Flipping breaks an utterance into two parts, and concatenate them in their reversed order. The break point is the punctuation that is closest to the middle of the utterance if there is any. Otherwise, we break the utterance at the middle.

As illustrated in Table 4, the proposed transformations neither change the implication of the contexts nor the appropriateness of the responses.

3 Data

We describe four datasets that we will be using to evaluate our proposed methods:

Taobao chat log was collected by a vendor of pajamas between 2013 and 2015. The conversations took place on Taobao, one of the largest Chinese e-commerce websites. The website allows two-way conversations between customers and agents in individual sessions.

Ubuntu dialog corpus (Lowe et al., 2015) is the first large dataset of online chats made available. It contains multi-party chat logs from Ubuntu chat room where people help each other to solve technical problems related to Ubuntu.

Douban conversation corpus is a collection of web forum post discussions from Douban, a Chinese internet community (Wu et al., 2016). It covers a wide range of topics, hence open-domain in nature.

Frames dataset was collected by (Asri et al., 2017) in wizard-of-oz setting. The chats are about booking flight. The wizard has access to database to answer domain-specific questions. Unlike the datasets mentioned above, the conversations of Frames are highly controlled so that the language is perfect and the chats have perfect turn exchanges.

4 Methodology

4.1 Model Overview

We first give a high level abstraction of the neural models we will be investigating. Given context and candidate responses, the models score each candidate and the one with the highest score is selected. The models are trained by maximizing the likelihood of labels. To build training data, one negative example is sampled from the corpus for each pair of context and true response. We group the models into the following two categories:

Dual-Encoder Model (DE) As first proposed in (Lowe et al., 2015), DE models encode context m and response r into $v(m) \in \mathbb{R}^l, v(r) \in \mathbb{R}^m$, respectively. Then

$$P(r \mid m) = \sigma(v(m)^T M v(r))$$

where σ is the sigmoid function, $M \in \mathbb{R}^{l \times m}$. In this paper, response encoder is LSTM. We consider two choices of context encoder: one is word-level LSTM encoder only (LSTM-DE), which takes concatenated messages as input. The other one is hierarchical recurrent encoder (HRE-DE). For HRE, we encode each message with an LSTM word-level encoder, and then feed the last hidden states from the word-level encoder to an utterance-level encoder, which is also an LSTM. We concatenate the last hidden state of the utterance-level encoder to that of word-level encoder on concatenated messages as final context encoding. Note that HRE-DE is a simplified version of the model in (Zhou et al., 2016).

Sequential Matching Network (SMN) Unlike DE models, SMN finds the affinity between context messages and responses as a first step (Wu et al., 2016). Given messages m_k where $k = 1, ..., n$ and response r, SMN first extract feature $u(m_k, r) \in \mathbb{R}^p$ of how related the two utterances are, and then accumulate these features with an

	Language	**Medium**	**Style**	**Domain**	**Size (Train)**	**Vocabulary**
Ubuntu	English	Chat Room	Noisy	Task	1M	400k
Taobao	Chinese	Chat Room	Noisy	Task	0.9M	90k
Douban	Chinese	Web Forum	Noisy	Open	1M	300k
Frames	English	Chat Room	Controlled	Task	11k	9k

Table 5: Comparison of four dialog corpora

RNN:

$$v(m, r) = RNN(u(m_k, r)), k = 1, ..., n$$

$$P(r \mid m) = \sigma(w^T v(m, r))$$

where $v(m, r), w \in \mathbb{R}^q$.

4.2 Combining Transformed Data

Let π_i be the applicable transformations including the identity. For context m and response r, let $m^i = \pi_i(m)$, $r^j = \pi_j(r)$. For DE models, we use the same encoder for m, r to encode m^i, r^j. Then we combine the encodings and predict by

$$P(r \mid m) = \sigma(\sum_{i,j} v(m^i)^T M_{ij} v(r^j))$$

where $M_{ij} \in \mathbb{R}^{l \times m}$. Similarly, for SMN, the predicted score is

$$P(r \mid m) = \sigma(\sum_{i,j} w_{i,j}^T v(m^i, r^j))$$

where $w_{i,j} \in \mathbb{R}^q$. Please note that this score function allows augmentations to be done at test time for prediction. Additionally, we inject squared distance between the encodings of the original data and the transformed data in order to enforce models to learn similar representations for them. We are assuming that the transformation should not drastically change the meanings of contexts and responses even though they are not exactly label-preserving. Empirically we found adding this regularization term actually helps. The training loss for DE models becomes

$$\sum_{(m,r)} (-\log P(r \mid m) + t(\sum_i \|v(m^i) - v(m)\|^2$$
$$+ \sum_j \|v(r^j) - v(r)\|^2)$$

and the one for SMN becomes

$$\sum_{(m,r)} (-\log P(r \mid m) + t(\sum_{i,j} \|v(m^i, r^j) - v(m, j)\|^2)$$

where t is a hyper-parameter. We tuned it on the validation set in $[0.01, 0.1]$.

5 Experiments

5.1 Setup

We evaluate our method on the datasets mentioned in Section 3. For the Ubuntu dataset, we use the version shared by (Xu et al., 2016). For Douban, we discard the test set provided by the authors since the responses are not from the same domain, and re-split training set. Negative responses are randomly sampled. For Frames, we select negative responses from those that have different slot types and values from true responses. We also conduct an experiment with smaller amount of training data on the three large datasets, Ubuntu, Douban, and Taobao, in which 1% of the training set are randomly selected for training. Following (Lowe et al., 2015), we evaluate the model performance with recall-at-1, following previous work.

We experiment with two types of permutation: the first one is permuting the last and the penultimate message in contexts, and the second one is permuting the penultimate with the third to last message. We only do the first type of permutation for SMN since SMN seems to be insensitive to permutation. We flip all messages in contexts and responses for SMN, and only flip context messages for DE models.

5.2 Training

We initialize word embeddings using the results of word2vec (Mikolov et al., 2013) trained on the whole corpus. The size of word embeddings is 300 for LSTM-DE and HRE-DE, and 200 for SMN. For LSTM-DE and HRE-DE, each LSTM layer has hidden size of 300. We use the same hyper-parameters for SMN as in (Wu et al., 2016). All models are trained with Adam optimizer with learning rate of 0.001. We use early stopping to choose parameters. For experiments on small training sets (including Frames), we additionally apply dropout (Srivastava et al., 2014) with rate 0.5 to all recurrent layers. As a side note, we find that dropout does not affect the result in any significant way under full-scale setting.

	Ubuntu		Taobao		Douban		Frames
	100%	1%	100%	1%	100%	1%	100%
LSTM-DE	0.6546	0.3470	0.8446	0.4862	0.6193	0.3301	0.3941
+ permutation 1	0.6773	0.3723	**0.8685**	0.5037	**0.6402**	**0.3503**	0.3973
+ permutation 2	**0.6854**	0.3685	**0.8693**	0.5071	**0.6469**	0.3444	0.4122
+ flipping	**0.6853**	0.3778	0.8669	0.5201	0.6430	0.3369	**0.4209**
HRE-DE	0.6729	0.3654	0.8728	0.5085	0.6443	0.3350	0.4436
+ permutation 1	0.6817	0.3650	0.8732	0.5053	0.6401	0.3423	0.4339
+ permutation 2	0.6786	**0.3713**	0.8787	**0.5207**	0.6430	0.3395	**0.4518**
+ flipping	**0.6920**	0.3688	**0.8828**	0.5147	**0.6542**	**0.3523**	**0.4564**
SMN	0.7050	0.4771	0.8194	0.5312	0.6700	0.4662	0.4055
+ permutation 1	0.7066	0.4749	0.8171	0.5302	0.6747	0.4669	0.4023
+ flipping	**0.7156**	**0.4893**	**0.8231**	**0.5387**	**0.6800**	**0.4876**	**0.4116**

Table 6: Numbers on recall-at-1. Best results for each dataset and each model are highlighted.

5.3 Main Results

Table 6 shows the performance of LSTM-DE, HRE-DE, and SMN on 4 different datasets under different types of augmentation. For each full-scale dataset, nearly all models gain around 1 to 3 points with one of the proposed data augmentation methods. Permutation works best for LSTM-DE, less so for HRE-DE, and has almost no effect on SMN. This is probably because HRE-DE and SMN have an utterance-level recurrent component which makes them better at capturing long range dependencies. Permutation 1 does not improve on Frames dataset for any model. This might be that Frames has perfect turn-taking, and wizards' responses are mostly addressing their immediately preceding messages, so moving away the last message in context does not help. In small-scale setting, LSTM-DE with data augmentation outperforms HRE-DE on some of the datasets. SMN gains even more with flipping than in full-scale setting.

6 Related Work

Data augmentation has been widely adopted in computer vision and speech recognition (Krizhevsky et al., 2012; Ko et al., 2015). In image processing, label-preserving transformations such as tilting and flipping are used, but in NLP, finding such transformations that exactly preserve meanings is difficult. Language data is discrete in nature, and minor perturbation may change the meaning. Most commonly used techniques include word substitution (Fadaee et al., 2017) and paraphrasing (Dong et al., 2017). These methods may require heavy external resources, which can be difficult to apply across multiple languages and domains.

Recently, there has been a surging interest in adversarial training (Goodfellow et al., 2014). For text data, one class of methods generate adversarial examples by moving word embeddings along the opposite direction of the gradient of loss functions (Wu et al., 2017; Yasunaga et al., 2017), hence small perturbation in the continuous space of word vectors. Another class of methods aim to create genuinely new examples. (Li et al., 2017) adds syntactic and semantic variations to training data based on grammar rules and thesaurus. (Xie et al., 2017) add noises to data by blanking out or substituting words for language modeling. (Yang et al., 2017) adopt a seq2seq model (Sutskever et al., 2014) to generate questions based on paragraphs and answers into their generative adversarial framework. One main difference between these methods and our approach is that, while adversarial training only manipulates training data, we in addition apply transformations to data *at test time* to help prediction. This is closer to (Dong et al., 2017) in spirit.

7 Conclusion

We proposed a general method to improve dialog response selection through manipulating existing data that can be applied to different models. Our results show that for both open-domain and task-oriented dialogues, and for both English and Chinese languages, at least one of the proposed augmentation methods is effective, and the chance that they hurt is rare. We have deliberately chosen a diverse set of domains and models to test this on to try to understand the contribution of data augmentation. Thus even when working on new datasets, and new models, it seems data augmentation is still a valuable addition that will likely improve results. Being more specific about when augmentation works is harder. One future research direction would be to apply data transformation situationally based on the discourse structure of dialogs. In our experiments, we tried combining permutation and flipping but found no advantage over using only one type of transformation. We believe a more sophisticated method of combination could further improve the results, and leave it to future work.

References

Yossi Adi, Einat Kermany, Yonatan Belinkov, Ofer Lavi, and Yoav Goldberg. 2016. Fine-grained analysis of sentence embeddings using auxiliary prediction tasks. *arXiv preprint arXiv:1608.04207*.

Layla El Asri, Hannes Schulz, Shikhar Sharma, Jeremie Zumer, Justin Harris, Emery Fine, Rahul Mehrotra, and Kaheer Suleman. 2017. Frames: A corpus for adding memory to goal-oriented dialogue systems. *arXiv preprint arXiv:1704.00057*.

Li Dong, Jonathan Mallinson, Siva Reddy, and Mirella Lapata. 2017. Learning to paraphrase for question answering. In *Proceedings of the 2017 Conference on Empirical Methods in Natural Language Processing*, pages 875–886.

Micha Elsner and Eugene Charniak. 2008. You talking to me? a corpus and algorithm for conversation disentanglement. *Proceedings of ACL-08: HLT*, pages 834–842.

Marzieh Fadaee, Arianna Bisazza, and Christof Monz. 2017. Data augmentation for low-resource neural machine translation. In *Proceedings of the 55th Annual Meeting of the Association for Computational Linguistics (Volume 2: Short Papers)*, volume 2, pages 567–573.

Ian J Goodfellow, Jonathon Shlens, and Christian Szegedy. 2014. Explaining and harnessing adversarial examples. *arXiv preprint arXiv:1412.6572*.

Urvashi Khandelwal, He He, Peng Qi, and Dan Jurafsky. 2018. Sharp nearby, fuzzy far away: How neural language models use context. *arXiv preprint arXiv:1805.04623*.

Tom Ko, Vijayaditya Peddinti, Daniel Povey, and Sanjeev Khudanpur. 2015. Audio augmentation for speech recognition. In *Sixteenth Annual Conference of the International Speech Communication Association*.

Alex Krizhevsky, Ilya Sutskever, and Geoffrey E Hinton. 2012. Imagenet classification with deep convolutional neural networks. In *Advances in neural information processing systems*, pages 1097–1105.

Yitong Li, Trevor Cohn, and Timothy Baldwin. 2017. Robust training under linguistic adversity. In *Proceedings of the 15th Conference of the European Chapter of the Association for Computational Linguistics: Volume 2, Short Papers*, volume 2, pages 21–27.

Ryan Lowe, Nissan Pow, Iulian Serban, and Joelle Pineau. 2015. The ubuntu dialogue corpus: A large dataset for research in unstructured multi-turn dialogue systems. *arXiv preprint arXiv:1506.08909*.

Tomas Mikolov, Ilya Sutskever, Kai Chen, Greg S Corrado, and Jeff Dean. 2013. Distributed representations of words and phrases and their compositionality. In *Advances in neural information processing systems*, pages 3111–3119.

Alan Ritter, Colin Cherry, and William B Dolan. 2011. Data-driven response generation in social media. In *Proceedings of the conference on empirical methods in natural language processing*, pages 583–593. Association for Computational Linguistics.

Nitish Srivastava, Geoffrey Hinton, Alex Krizhevsky, Ilya Sutskever, and Ruslan Salakhutdinov. 2014. Dropout: A simple way to prevent neural networks from overfitting. *The Journal of Machine Learning Research*, 15(1):1929–1958.

Ilya Sutskever, Oriol Vinyals, and Quoc V Le. 2014. Sequence to sequence learning with neural networks. In *Advances in neural information processing systems*, pages 3104–3112.

Yi Wu, David Bamman, and Stuart Russell. 2017. Adversarial training for relation extraction. In *Proceedings of the 2017 Conference on Empirical Methods in Natural Language Processing*, pages 1778–1783.

Yu Wu, Wei Wu, Chen Xing, Ming Zhou, and Zhoujun Li. 2016. Sequential matching network: A new architecture for multi-turn response selection in retrieval-based chatbots. *arXiv preprint arXiv:1612.01627*.

Ziang Xie, Sida I Wang, Jiwei Li, Daniel Lévy, Aiming Nie, Dan Jurafsky, and Andrew Y Ng. 2017. Data noising as smoothing in neural network language models. *arXiv preprint arXiv:1703.02573*.

Zhen Xu, Bingquan Liu, Baoxun Wang, Chengjie Sun, and Xiaolong Wang. 2016. Incorporating loose-structured knowledge into lstm with recall gate for conversation modeling. *arXiv preprint arXiv:1605.05110*.

Zhilin Yang, Junjie Hu, Ruslan Salakhutdinov, and William W Cohen. 2017. Semi-supervised qa with generative domain-adaptive nets. *arXiv preprint arXiv:1702.02206*.

Michihiro Yasunaga, Jungo Kasai, and Dragomir Radev. 2017. Robust multilingual part-of-speech tagging via adversarial training. *arXiv preprint arXiv:1711.04903*.

Xiangyang Zhou, Daxiang Dong, Hua Wu, Shiqi Zhao, Dianhai Yu, Hao Tian, Xuan Liu, and Rui Yan. 2016. Multi-view response selection for human-computer conversation. In *Proceedings of the 2016 Conference on Empirical Methods in Natural Language Processing*, pages 372–381.

A Knowledge-Grounded Multimodal Search-Based Conversational Agent

Shubham Agarwal *, Ondřej Dušek, Ioannis Konstas and Verena Rieser
The Interaction Lab, Department of Computer Science
Heriot-Watt University, Edinburgh, UK
* Adeptmind Scholar, Adeptmind Inc., Toronto, Canada
`{sa201, o.dusek, i.konstas, v.t.rieser}@hw.ac.uk`

Abstract

Multimodal search-based dialogue is a challenging new task: It extends visually grounded question answering systems into multi-turn conversations with access to an external database. We address this new challenge by learning a neural response generation system from the recently released Multimodal Dialogue (MMD) dataset (Saha et al., 2017). We introduce a knowledge-grounded multimodal conversational model where an encoded knowledge base (KB) representation is appended to the decoder input. Our model substantially outperforms strong baselines in terms of text-based similarity measures (over 9 BLEU points, 3 of which are solely due to the use of additional information from the KB).

1 Introduction

Conversational agents have become ubiquitous, with variants ranging from open-domain conversational chit-chat bots (Ram et al., 2018; Papaioannou et al., 2017; Fang et al., 2017) to domain-specific task-based dialogue systems (Singh et al., 2000; Rieser and Lemon, 2010, 2011; Young et al., 2013; Wen et al., 2017).

Our work builds upon the recently released Multimodal Dialogue (MMD) dataset (Saha et al., 2017), which contains dialogue sessions in the e-commerce (fashion) domain. Figure 1 illustrates an example chat session with multimodal interaction between the user and the system. We focus on the task of generating textual responses conditioned on the previous conversational history. Traditional goal-oriented dialogue systems relied on slot-filling approach to this task, i.e. explicit modelling of all attributes in the domain (Lemon

et al., 2006; Wang and Lemon, 2013; Young et al., 2013). On the other hand, previous work on MMD data used direct learning from raw texts with implicit semantic representation only. This paper attempts to combine both approaches by learning to generate replies from raw user input, while also incorporating Knowledge Base (KB) inputs (i.e. explicit semantics) into the generation process. We discuss how our model is able to handle various user intents (request types) and the impact of incorporating the additional explicit semantic information from the KB into particular targeted intents. We use user intent annotation and KB queries provided with the dataset for the purpose of this work.

Our main contribution is the resulting fully data-driven model for the task of conversational multimodal dialogue generation, grounded in conversational text history, vision and KB inputs. We also illustrate a method to improve context modelling over multiple images and show great improvements over the baseline. Finally, we present a detailed analysis of the outputs generated by our system corresponding to different user intents.

2 Related Work

With recent progress in deep learning, there is continued interest in the tasks involving both vision and language, such as image captioning (Xu et al., 2015; Vinyals et al., 2015; Karpathy and Fei-Fei, 2015), visual storytelling (Huang et al., 2016), video description (Venugopalan et al., 2015b,a) or dialogue grounded in visual context (Antol et al., 2015; Das et al., 2017; Tapaswi et al., 2016).

Bordes et al. (2016) and Ghazvininejad et al. (2017) presented knowledge-grounded neural models; however, these are uni-modal in nature, involve only textual interaction and do not take into account the conversational history in a dia-

59

Proceedings of the 2018 EMNLP Workshop SCAI: The 2nd Int'l Workshop on Search-Oriented Conversational AI, pages 59–66
Brussels, Belgium, October 31, 2018. ©2018 Association for Computational Linguistics

U1   **SHOPPER:** Hi there

A1   **AGENT:** Hi, anything i can help you with today?

U2   **SHOPPER:** I am here to shop for tapered type casual trousers that my brother would like .

U3   **SHOPPER:** he is 26 years of age.

A2   **AGENT:** Oh. Good

A3   **AGENT:** let me just make a quick search through my catalogue

A4   **AGENT:**

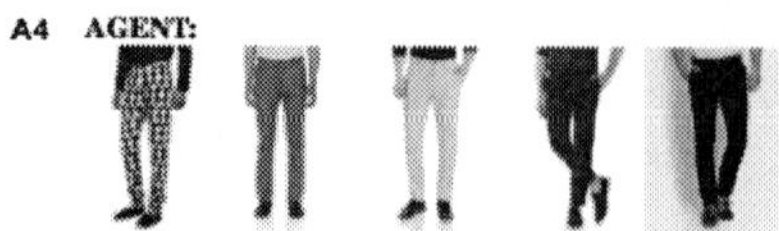

U4   **SHOPPER:** Are the products in the 5th, 1st and 2nd images suited for multicoloured pocketted?

A5   **AGENT:** Yes

U5   **SHOPPER:** And for melange?

A6   **AGENT:** No

U6   **SHOPPER:** Show me more images of the 3rd product in some different directions

A7   **AGENT:** Sorry i couldnt find any other orientations for this image

U7   **SHOPPER:** I dont like the 4th image . Show me something in fit as in this image

Figure 1: Example chatlog depicting multimodal user-agent interaction in a dialogue session from the MMD dataset. The system needs to ground knowledge to generate responses related to product-specific attributes. We focus on textual response generation given a fixed-size conversational history.

logue. In contrast, our system grounds on a KB while also conditioning on previous dialogue context which is multimodal in nature, consisting of both textual and visual communication between the user and the system. We formulate our KB input from a database query (triggered by the system) similar to Sha et al. (2018), as described in Section 3.2.

Our model belongs to the encoder-decoder paradigm where sequence-to-sequence models (Cho et al., 2014; Sutskever et al., 2014; Bahdanau et al., 2015) have become the de-facto standard for natural language generation. However, they tend to ignore the conversational history in a dialogue. The Hierarchical Recurrent Encoder Decoder (HRED) architecture (Serban et al., 2016, 2017; Lu et al., 2016) addresses this limitation by using a context recurrent neural network (RNN), forming a hierarchical encoder. We build upon these HRED models and refer to them as Text-only HREDs (T-HRED) in the following. Our model is most similar to the Multimodal HRED (M-HRED) of Saha et al. (2017), with context and KB exten-

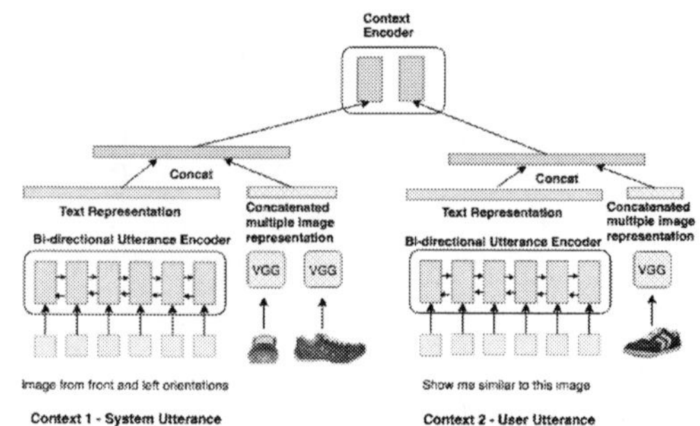

Figure 2: Schematic diagram of hierarchical encoder described in Section 3.1. Figure 3 depicts full pipeline of the model using knowledge base input. In contrast to Saha et al. (2017), we model over multiple images in a contextual dialogue turn by combining all 'local' representations of multiple images to a 'global' image representation per turn. We show a context of 2 turns for simplicity.

sions (see Section 3).

3   Knowledge grounded Multimodal Conversational model

While Saha et al. (2017) propose Multimodal HRED (M-HRED) by extending T-HRED to include visual context over images, they do not ground their dialogue context over an external database. Also, they limit the visual information by 'unrolling' multiple images to just use the last image of a single turn. For example in Figure 1, Saha et al. (2017) consider only the last image of trousers as visual context in Agent's response A4. In contrast, we include all the images in a single turn using a linear layer (see Agarwal et al. (2018) for a detailed analysis).

In addition, we devise a mechanism to ground our textual responses on a KB; Figure 3 depicts the full pipeline of our model. We combine textual and visual representations at the encoder level and pass it through the HRED's context encoder (cf. Figure 2), which learns the backbone of the conversation (see Section 3.1). Subsequently, we inject knowledge from the KB at the decoder level in each timestep (see Sections 3.2 and 3.3).

Formally, we model a dialogue as a sequence of utterances (turns) which are considered as sequences of words and images:

$$P_\theta(t_1, \ldots t_N) = \prod_{n=1}^{N} P_\theta(t_n | t_{<n}) \qquad (1)$$

Here t_n represents the n-th utterance in a dialogue.

60

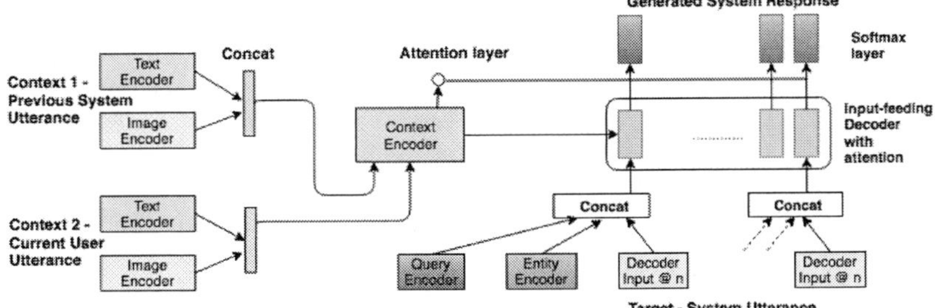

Figure 3: The full encoder-decoder pipeline of our model. While we have early fusion of textual and image representations (which act as input to the context encoder, see Figure 2), we employ late fusion of the knowledge base vector at the decoder level. For simplicity, we show a context of 2 turns.

The whole model is trained using cross entropy on next-word prediction:

$$J(\theta) = -\sum_{n=1}^{N} \log P(y_n | y_0 \ldots y_{t-1}) \quad (2)$$

In the following, we explain all the different components of our model. We use the following notation: $f_\theta^{text}, f_\theta^{cxt}, f_\theta^{query}, f_\theta^{ent}$ and f_θ^{dec} are all GRU cells (Cho et al., 2014) and g_θ^{enc} is a Convolutional Neural Network (CNN) image encoder. θ represent our model weights. $w_{n,m}$ is the m-th word in the n-th textual utterance. Similarly, $q_{m,n}$ and $c_{m,n}$ represent input at each timestep in the query and entity encoder (see Section 3.2).

3.1 Hierarchical Encoder

The encoder is formed of the following modules:

Utterance (Text) encoder: We pass each utterance (previous system responses as well as current user query) in a given context through a text encoder. We use bidirectional GRU (f_θ^{text}) to generate the textual representation h_{n,M_n}^{text} (cf. Eq. (3)). These textual representations are combined with image representations in each turn, forming the input for the context encoder.

$$h_{n,m}^{text} = f_\theta^{text}(h_{n,m-1}^{text}, w_{m,n}); \quad h_{n,0}^{text} = 0 \quad (3)$$

Image encoder: We first extract the 'local' image representations for all images in a dialogue turn (denoted by $g_\theta^{enc}(img_k)$ in Eq. (4)) and concatenate them together.[1] This concatenated vector is passed through a linear layer to form the 'global' image context for a single turn, denoted by h_n^{img}.

$$h_n^{img} = l^{img}([g_\theta^{enc}(img_1), \ldots g_\theta^{enc}(img_k)]) \quad (4)$$

[1]We used the VGGnet (Simonyan and Zisserman, 2015) CNN to obtain the local image representations. Since the number of images in a turn is ≤ 5, we consider zero vectors in the absence of images.

Context encoder: The final hidden representations from both text encoder h_{n,M_n}^{text} and image encoder h_n^{img} are concatenated for each turn and serve as input to the context RNN (cf. Eq. (5)). On top of the text and image encoder, this builds a hierarchical encoder modelling the dialogue history. The final hidden state of the context RNN h_N^{cxt} acts as the initial state of the decoder RNN defined in Section 3.3.

$$h_n^{cxt} = f_\theta^{cxt}(h_{n-1}^{cxt}, [h_{n,M_n}^{text}, h_n^{img}]); \quad h_0^{cxt} = 0 \quad (5)$$

3.2 Knowledge base (KB) input

The KB vector h_n^{kb} in Eq. (8) is formed by concatenating the h_n^{query} and h_n^{ent} representations. While our approach is modelled around the MMD dataset which provides contextual KB queries and profiles of celebrities endorsing specific products, it can be applied to other KBs with encoded queries and (optionally) properties of relevant entities.

$$h_n^{query} = f_\theta^{query}(h_{n-1}^{query}, q_{m,n}) \quad (6)$$
$$h_n^{ent} = f_\theta^{ent}(h_{n-1}^{ent}, c_{m,n}) \quad (7)$$
$$h_n^{kb} = [h_n^{query}, h_n^{ent}] \quad (8)$$
$$h_0^{query} = 0; \quad h_0^{ent} = 0 \quad (9)$$

Query encoder: Each chat session contains multiple queries to the database which retrieve the relevant product suited to user requirements at specific turn. We replicate this query for subsequent dialogue turns until a new query is triggered by the system. This query acts as knowledge base for the model at each turn. We show a sample input to the model in Figure 4. We used unidirectional GRU cell to encode the query input h_n^{query}.

Entity encoder: The input to the entity encoder is a list of entities relevant to the query at hand (see Figure 5). GRU cells are used to produce the resulting h_n^{ent}. Specifically, the MMD dataset categorises products into synonym sets (synsets) and

61

Query:
```
"search_criteria": {
    "name": {"driving shoes": 1.0},
    "fit":{"tight": 1.0},
    "brand": {"cirohuner": 1.0},
    "image_type":{"front": 1.0},
    "gender": {"men": 1.0},
    "print": {"chain": 1.0}
}
```
Knowledge base input:
```
name driving shoes fit tight brand
cirohuner image_type front gender
men print chain
```

Figure 4: Sample query to the database and corresponding knowledge base input vector.

1.
```
User: what kind of trousers are
endorsed by celebrity cel_237?
Intent: celebrity
Subintent :does_celebrity_endorse_n
Celebrity: cel_237
Celebrity input: boxer briefs
```
2.
```
User: which of the celebrities
usually wear similar looking canvas
shoes as in the 2nd image
Intent: celebrity
Subintent: which_celebrity_endorses_n
Synset: canvas shoes
Celebrity input:
cel_987 cel_2 cel_316 cel_101
```

Figure 5: Two input scenarios for the entity encoder depending on the fine grained user intent. If there is no 'celebrity' intent, we have an empty string as input to the entity encoder.

provides a list of celebrities endorsing each synset (see Section 4.1 for details).

This input is used specifically for the 'celebrity' intent in our model, where the user asks about celebrities endorsing a product. For each target prediction with celebrity intent, we first extract the relevant celebrity profiles using basic pattern matching over the user utterance. For each of the celebrities in the user query, we order the corresponding synsets by their probability of endorsement. If no celebrity is found, we use synset information from the query to extract celebrities which endorse the corresponding synset.

3.3   Input feeding decoder

We use an input feeding decoder with the attention mechanism of Luong et al. (2015). We concatenate the KB input h_n^{kb} with the decoder input (cf. Eq. (10), where $h_{n,0}^{dec} = h_N^{cxt}$). The rationale behind this late fusion of KB representation is that KB input remains the same for a given context and

does not change on each turn. On the other hand, images and textual response together form a context in a dialogue turn and thus we fuse them early at the encoder level. The decoder is trained using cross-entropy loss defined in Eq. (2).

$$h_{n,m}^{dec} = f_\theta^{dec}(h_{n,m-1}^{dec}, w_{n,m}, h_{n-1}^{cxt}, h_{n-1}^{kb}) \quad (10)$$

4   Experiments and Results

4.1   Dataset

Our work is based on the Multimodal Dialogue (MMD) dataset (Saha et al., 2017), which consists of 150k chat sessions.[2] User queries can be complex from the perspective of multimodal task-specific dialogue, such as "Show me more images of the 3rd product in some different directions". However, it also heavily relies on the external KB to answer product attributes related to user queries, such as "What is the brand/material of the suit in 3rd image?" or "Show something similar to 1st result but in a different material". This dataset contains raw chat logs as well as metadata information of the corresponding products. Around 400 anonymised celebrity profiles have been introduced in the system to emulate endorsement in recommendation, such as "What kind of slippers are endorsed by cel_145?". For each dialogue turn, there are manual annotations of the user intent available. We use the intents to construct celebrity encodings. On average, each session contains 40 dialogue turns. The system response depends on the intent state of the user query and on average contains 8 words and 4 images per utterance. We created our own version of the dataset from the raw chat logs of the dialogue session and metadata information. As discussed in Section 3.1, this was necessary to model the visual context over multiple images. We created the KB input to our model as described in Section 3.2 from the raw chat logs and the metadata information.

4.2   Implementation

We used PyTorch[3] (Paszke et al., 2017) for our experiments.[4] We did not use any kind of delexicalisation[5] and rely on our model to directly learn

---

[2]We used the same training-development-test split as provided by the dataset authors.

[3]https://pytorch.org/

[4]Code can be found at:
https://github.com/shubhamagarwal92/mmd

[5]Replacing specific values with placeholders (Henderson et al., 2014).

from the conversational history and KB. All encoders and decoders are based on 1-layer GRU cells (Cho et al., 2014) with 512 as the hidden state size. We used the 4096 dimensional FC6 layer image representations from VGG-19 (Simonyan and Zisserman, 2015) provided by Saha et al. (2017). Adam (Kingma and Ba, 2015) was chosen as the optimizer, and we clipped gradients greater than 5. We experimented with different learning rates and settled on the value of 0.0004. Dropout of 0.3 is applied to all the RNN cells to avoid overfitting, and we perform early stopping by tracking the validation loss (with single trial for each experiment).

4.3 Analysis and Results

We evaluate our response generation using the BLEU (Papineni et al., 2002), METEOR (Lavie and Agarwal, 2007) and ROUGE-L (Lin and Och, 2004) automatic metrics.[6] We reproduce the baseline results from Saha et al. (2017) using their code and data-generation scripts.[7]

Model	Cxt	BLEU-4	METEOR	ROUGE-L
Saha et al. M-HRED*	2	0.3767	0.2847	0.6235
T-HRED	2	0.4292	0.3269	0.6692
M-HRED	2	0.4308	0.3288	0.6700
T-HRED–attn	2	0.4331	0.3298	0.6710
M-HRED–attn	2	0.4345	0.3315	0.6712
T-HRED–attn	5	0.4442	0.3374	0.6797
M-HRED–attn	5	0.4451	0.3371	0.6799
M-HRED–kb	2	0.4573	0.3436	0.6872
T-HRED–attn–kb	2	0.4601	0.3456	0.6909
M-HRED–attn–kb	2	0.4624	0.3476	0.6917
T-HRED–attn–kb	5	0.4612	0.3461	0.6913
M-HRED–attn–kb	5	**0.4634**	**0.3480**	**0.6923**

Table 1: Automated evaluation based on BLEU-4, METEOR and ROUGE-L metrics. Here, 'M' represents multimodality while 'T' stands for text-only model. 'attn' denotes use of attention and 'kb' signifies incorporating Knowledge Base input. 'Cxt' represents context size for the dialogue history.
*Saha et al. was trained on a different version of the dataset, as discussed in Section 3.

Table 1 summarises the results for our M-HRED model without incorporating KB information. Attention-based models consistently outperform their counterparts. Adding the visual inputs does not lead to major improvements (M-HRED vs. T-HRED for a given context). However,

Intent	Model	BLEU-4
show-similar-to	M-HRED–attn	0.9998
	M-HRED–attn–kb	1.0
sort-results	M-HRED–attn	0.9188
	M-HRED–attn–kb	0.9384
suited-for	M-HRED–attn	0.6151
	M-HRED–attn–kb	0.6216
show-orientation	M-HRED–attn	0.5388
	M-HRED–attn–kb	0.5854
buy	M-HRED–attn	0.2665
	M-HRED–attn–kb	0.3179
ask-attribute	M-HRED–attn	0.4960
	M-HRED–attn–kb	0.5934
celebrity	M-HRED–attn	0.2671
	M-HRED–attn–kb	0.2725

Table 2: BLEU scores for the entire corpus predictions for specific intents with a context of 5.

grounding in KB gave a stark uplift (M-HRED–attn–kb vs. M-HRED–attn) for a given context size. Adding KB input boosts performance more for a shorter context compared to longer context. It can be conjectured that the longer context contains some of the information that is in the KB queries and so there is less impact of the KB input when we include the longer context. Compare the difference for M-HRED–attn–kb vs. M-HRED–attn for a context of 2 (3 BLEU points) vs. 5 (2 BLEU points) in Table 1. Conversely, longer context improves more the models without KB queries.

In summary, our best performing model (M-HRED–attn–kb) outperforms the model of Saha et al. (2017) by 9 BLEU points. We also analysed our generated outputs for different user intents, as shown in Table 2. As assumed, intents such as 'show-similar-to' and 'sort-results' are relatively easy from the perspective of NLG, requiring no information about the product description; our model matches the reference almost perfectly.

We found great improvements for the 'ask-attribute' intent where the KB-grounded model could answer correctly questions related to brand or colour and other attributes of the product, which resulted in an increase of 10 BLEU points on test instances with this user intent (M-HRED–attn–kb compared to M-HRED–attn). Similarly, in the example related to the 'buy' intent in Table 3, our model is able to learn that the product bought by the user is 'kurta', which probably cannot be captured by the visual features. Hence, M-HRED–attn produces 'jeans' on the output. M-HRED–attn–kb on the other hand learns this information from the KB. We also found that our BLEU score for the 'show-orientation' intent has decreased w.r.t. to the non-KB-grounded model. A detailed

---

[6] We used the evaluation scripts provided by (Sharma et al., 2017).
[7] https://github.com/amritasaha1812/MMD_Code

Intent	Model	Example Text
show-similar-to		**Text context**: yes. | show me something similar to the 1st image but in a different material **Gold Target**: the similar looking ones are **KB**: *name[casual-trousers] gender[women] brand[antigravity] synsets[casual-trousers]*
	M-HRED–attn	**Predicted**: the similar looking ones are
	M-HRED–attn–kb	**Predicted**: the similar looking ones are
sort-results		**Text context**: sorry i dont seem to have anything in loop but would you like in slim | sort these by best seller ranking **Gold Target**: sorry i do not have the best seller ranking information for these **KB**: *name[casual-trousers] gender[women] brand[antigravity] synsets[casual-trousers]*
	M-HRED–attn	**Predicted**: sorry i dont have the best seller ranking information for the rest
	M-HRED–attn–kb	**Predicted**: sorry i do not have the best seller ranking information for these
suited-for		**Text context**: no. | which care might go well with this dupatta? **Gold Target**: it will suit well for professional and handwash care **KB**: *name[dupatta] gender[women] synsets[dupatta] image-type[front] care[handwash]*
	M-HRED–attn	**Predicted**: it will suit well for gentle hand care
	M-HRED–attn–kb	**Predicted**: it will suit well for *hand wash care*
show-orientation		**Text context**: | show me more images of the 3rd product from some different orientations **Gold Target**: sorry i couldnt find any other orientations for this image **KB**: *name[casual-trousers] gender[women] brand[antigravity] synsets[casual-trousers]*
	M-HRED–attn	**Predicted**: image from the front, right, back and left orientations respectively
	M-HRED–attn–kb	**Predicted**: sorry i couldnt find any other orientations for this image
buy		**Text context**: | i like the 4th one. i think ill buy that one **Gold Target**: absolutely , thats a great kurta **KB**: *name [kurta] color [green] gender [men] synsets [kurta] image-type [front]*
	M-HRED–attn	**Predicted**: absolutely , i think thats a great jeans
	M-HRED–attn–kb	**Predicted**: absolutely , i think thats a great *kurta*
ask-attribute		**Text context**: yes. | what is the brand in the 1st result? **Gold Target**: the blouse in the 1st image has alfani brand **KB**: *name [blouse] brand [alfani] synsets [blouse] image-type [look] gender [women]*
	M-HRED–attn	**Predicted**: the brand in 1st image is topshop
	M-HRED–attn–kb	**Predicted**: the brand in 1st image is *alfani*
celebrity		**Text context**: yes. celebrities cel_779, cel_10 and cel_513 also endorse this type of cufflinks | and celebrity cel_603 for the 1st? **Gold Target**: yes **KB Query**: *name[casual-trousers] gender[women] synsets[casual-trousers]* **KB Entity**: *scarf earrings casual trousers casual shirt*
	M-HRED–attn	**Predicted**: no.
	M-HRED–attn–kb	**Predicted**: yes.

Table 3: Examples of predictions corresponding to different user intents, showcasing the effect of grounding in KB. We show textual context as well as relevant knowledge base input (and omit image context) for brevity's sake. While our model uses a context of 5, for simplicity, we show only 2 previous turns.

probe found that the orientations for retrieved images may not directly follow the description in the query (KB). There are other intents for which even KB does not help, such as those requiring user modelling.

5 Conclusion and Future Work

This work focuses on the task of textual response generation in multimodal task-oriented dialogue system. We used the recently released Multimodal Dialogue (MMD) dataset (Saha et al., 2017) for experiments and introduced a novel conversational model grounded in language, vision and Knowledge Base (KB). Our best performing model outperforms the baseline model (Saha et al., 2017) by 9 BLEU points, improving context modelling in multimodal dialogue generation. Even though our

model outputs showed a substantial improvement (over 3 BLEU points) on incorporating KB information, integrating visual context still remains a bottleneck, as also observed by Agrawal et al. (2016); Qian et al. (2018). This suggests the need for a better mechanism to encode visual context.

Since our KB-grounded model assumes user intent annotation and KB queries as additional inputs, we plan to build a model to provide them automatically.

Acknowledgments

This research received funding from Adeptmind Inc., Montreal, Canada and the MaDrIgAL EPSRC project (EP/N017536/1). The Titan Xp used for this work was donated by the NVIDIA Corp.

References

Shubham Agarwal, Ondřej Dušek, Ioannis Konstas, and Verena Rieser. 2018. Improving context modelling in multimodal dialogue generation. In *Proc. INLG*. To appear.

Aishwarya Agrawal, Dhruv Batra, and Devi Parikh. 2016. Analyzing the behavior of visual question answering models. In *Proc. EMNLP*, pages 1955–1960.

Stanislaw Antol, Aishwarya Agrawal, Jiasen Lu, Margaret Mitchell, Dhruv Batra, C Lawrence Zitnick, and Devi Parikh. 2015. VQA: Visual question answering. In *Proc. ICCV*, pages 2425–2433.

Dzmitry Bahdanau, Kyunghyun Cho, and Yoshua Bengio. 2015. Neural machine translation by jointly learning to align and translate. In *Proc. ICLR*.

Antoine Bordes, Y-Lan Boureau, and Jason Weston. 2016. Learning end-to-end goal-oriented dialog. *CoRR abs/1605.07683*.

Kyunghyun Cho, Bart Van Merriënboer, Caglar Gulcehre, Dzmitry Bahdanau, Fethi Bougares, Holger Schwenk, and Yoshua Bengio. 2014. Learning phrase representations using RNN encoder-decoder for statistical machine translation. In *Proc. EMNLP*, pages 1724–1734.

Abhishek Das, Satwik Kottur, Khushi Gupta, Avi Singh, Deshraj Yadav, José MF Moura, Devi Parikh, and Dhruv Batra. 2017. Visual dialog. In *Proc. ICCV*, volume 2.

Hao Fang, Hao Cheng, Elizabeth Clark, Ariel Holtzman, Maarten Sap, Mari Ostendorf, Yejin Choi, and Noah A Smith. 2017. Sounding Board–University of Washington's Alexa Prize submission. In *Alexa Prize Proceedings*.

Marjan Ghazvininejad, Chris Brockett, Ming-Wei Chang, Bill Dolan, Jianfeng Gao, Wen-tau Yih, and Michel Galley. 2017. A knowledge-grounded neural conversation model. *CoRR abs/1702.01932*.

M. Henderson, B. Thomson, and S. Young. 2014. Robust dialog state tracking using delexicalised recurrent neural networks and unsupervised adaptation. In *IEEE Spoken Language Technology Workshop (SLT)*, pages 360–365.

Ting-Hao Kenneth Huang, Francis Ferraro, Nasrin Mostafazadeh, Ishan Misra, Aishwarya Agrawal, Jacob Devlin, Ross Girshick, Xiaodong He, Pushmeet Kohli, Dhruv Batra, Lawrence C. Zitnick, Devi Parikh, Lucy Vanderwende, Michel Galley, and Margaret Mitchell. 2016. Visual storytelling. *Proc. NAACL*, pages 1233–1239.

Andrej Karpathy and Li Fei-Fei. 2015. Deep visual-semantic alignments for generating image descriptions. In *Proc. ICCV*, pages 3128–3137.

Diederik P Kingma and Jimmy Ba. 2015. Adam: A method for stochastic optimization. In *Proc. ICLR*.

Alon Lavie and Abhaya Agarwal. 2007. METEOR: An automatic metric for MT evaluation with high levels of correlation with human judgments. In *Proc. 2nd Workshop on Statistical Machine Translation*, pages 228–231.

Oliver Lemon, Kallirroi Georgila, James Henderson, and Matthew Stuttle. 2006. An ISU dialogue system exhibiting reinforcement learning of dialogue policies: generic slot-filling in the talk in-car system. In *Proc. EACL*, pages 119–122.

Chin-Yew Lin and Franz Josef Och. 2004. Automatic evaluation of machine translation quality using longest common subsequence and skip-bigram statistics. In *Proc. ACL*, page 605.

Jiasen Lu, Jianwei Yang, Dhruv Batra, and Devi Parikh. 2016. Hierarchical question-image co-attention for visual question answering. In *Proc. NIPS*, pages 289–297.

Minh-Thang Luong, Hieu Pham, and Christopher D Manning. 2015. Effective approaches to attention-based neural machine translation. *Proc. EMNLP*, pages 1412–1421.

Ioannis Papaioannou, Amanda Cercas Curry, Jose L Part, Igor Shalyminov, Xinnuo Xu, Yanchao Yu, Ondrej Dušek, Verena Rieser, and Oliver Lemon. 2017. Alana: Social dialogue using an ensemble model and a ranker trained on user feedback. *Alexa Prize Proceedings*.

Kishore Papineni, Salim Roukos, Todd Ward, and Wei-Jing Zhu. 2002. BLEU: a method for automatic evaluation of machine translation. In *Proc. ACL*, pages 311–318.

Adam Paszke, Sam Gross, Soumith Chintala, Gregory Chanan, Edward Yang, Zachary DeVito, Zeming Lin, Alban Desmaison, Luca Antiga, and Adam Lerer. 2017. Automatic differentiation in PyTorch. In *NIPS-W*.

Xin Qian, Ziyi Zhong, and Jieli Zhou. 2018. Multimodal machine translation with reinforcement learning. *CoRR abs/1805.02356*.

Ashwin Ram, Rohit Prasad, Chandra Khatri, Anu Venkatesh, Raefer Gabriel, Qing Liu, Jeff Nunn, Behnam Hedayatnia, Ming Cheng, Ashish Nagar, et al. 2018. Conversational AI: The science behind the Alexa Prize. *CoRR abs/1801.03604*.

Verena Rieser and Oliver Lemon. 2010. Natural language generation as planning under uncertainty for spoken dialogue systems. In *Empirical methods in natural language generation*, pages 105–120. Springer.

Verena Rieser and Oliver Lemon. 2011. *Reinforcement learning for adaptive dialogue systems: a data-driven methodology for dialogue management and natural language generation.* Springer.

Amrita Saha, Mitesh Khapra, and Karthik Sankaranarayanan. 2017. Multimodal dialogs (MMD): A large-scale dataset for studying multimodal domain-aware conversations. *CoRR abs/1704.00200.*

Iulian Vlad Serban, Alessandro Sordoni, Yoshua Bengio, Aaron C Courville, and Joelle Pineau. 2016. Building end-to-end dialogue systems using generative hierarchical neural network models. In *Proc. AAAI*, pages 3776–3783.

Iulian Vlad Serban, Alessandro Sordoni, Ryan Lowe, Laurent Charlin, Joelle Pineau, Aaron C Courville, and Yoshua Bengio. 2017. A hierarchical latent variable encoder-decoder model for generating dialogues. In *Proc. AAAI*, pages 3295–3301.

Lei Sha, Lili Mou, Tianyu Liu, Pascal Poupart, Sujian Li, Baobao Chang, and Zhifang Sui. 2018. Order-planning neural text generation from structured data. *Proc. AAAI.*

Shikhar Sharma, Layla El Asri, Hannes Schulz, and Jeremie Zumer. 2017. Relevance of unsupervised metrics in task-oriented dialogue for evaluating natural language generation. *CoRR abs/1706.09799.*

Karen Simonyan and Andrew Zisserman. 2015. Very deep convolutional networks for large-scale image recognition. *Proc. ICLR.*

Satinder P Singh, Michael J Kearns, Diane J Litman, and Marilyn A Walker. 2000. Reinforcement learning for spoken dialogue systems. In *Proc. NIPS*, pages 956–962.

Ilya Sutskever, Oriol Vinyals, and Quoc V Le. 2014. Sequence to sequence learning with neural networks. In *Proc. NIPS*, pages 3104–3112.

Makarand Tapaswi, Yukun Zhu, Rainer Stiefelhagen, Antonio Torralba, Raquel Urtasun, and Sanja Fidler. 2016. MovieQA: Understanding stories in movies through question-answering. In *Proc. CVPR*, pages 4631–4640.

Subhashini Venugopalan, Marcus Rohrbach, Jeffrey Donahue, Raymond Mooney, Trevor Darrell, and Kate Saenko. 2015a. Sequence to sequence-video to text. In *Proc. ICCV*, pages 4534–4542.

Subhashini Venugopalan, Huijuan Xu, Jeff Donahue, Marcus Rohrbach, Raymond Mooney, and Kate Saenko. 2015b. Translating videos to natural language using deep recurrent neural networks. *Proc. NAACL*, pages 1494–1504.

Oriol Vinyals, Alexander Toshev, Samy Bengio, and Dumitru Erhan. 2015. Show and tell: A neural image caption generator. In *Proc. CVPR*, pages 3156–3164.

Zhuoran Wang and Oliver Lemon. 2013. A simple and generic belief tracking mechanism for the dialog state tracking challenge: On the believability of observed information. In *Proc. SIGDIAL*, pages 423–432.

Tsung-Hsien Wen, David Vandyke, Nikola Mrksic, Milica Gasic, Lina M Rojas-Barahona, Pei-Hao Su, Stefan Ultes, and Steve Young. 2017. A network-based end-to-end trainable task-oriented dialogue system. In *Proc. EACL*, pages 438–449.

Kelvin Xu, Jimmy Ba, Ryan Kiros, Kyunghyun Cho, Aaron Courville, Ruslan Salakhudinov, Rich Zemel, and Yoshua Bengio. 2015. Show, attend and tell: Neural image caption generation with visual attention. In *Proc. ICML*, pages 2048–2057.

Steve Young, Milica Gašić, Blaise Thomson, and Jason D Williams. 2013. POMDP-based statistical spoken dialog systems: A review. *Proceedings of the IEEE*, 101(5):1160–1179.

Embedding Individual Table Columns for Resilient SQL Chatbots

Bojan Petrovski[†1], Ignacio Aguado[‡1], Andreea Hossmann[‡], Michael Baeriswyl[‡], Claudiu Musat[‡]
† School of Computer and Communication Sciences, EPFL, Switzerland
‡ Artificial Intelligence Group - Swisscom AG
firstname.lastname@{epfl.ch, swisscom.com}

Abstract

Most of the world's data is stored in relational databases. Accessing these requires specialized knowledge of the Structured Query Language (SQL), putting them out of the reach of many people. A recent research thread in Natural Language Processing (NLP) aims to alleviate this problem by automatically translating natural language questions into SQL queries. While the proposed solutions are a great start, they lack robustness and do not easily generalize: the methods require high quality descriptions of the database table columns, and the most widely used training dataset, WikiSQL, is heavily biased towards using those descriptions as part of the questions.

In this work, we propose solutions to both problems: we entirely eliminate the need for column descriptions, by relying solely on their contents, and we augment the WikiSQL dataset by paraphrasing column names to reduce bias. We show that the accuracy of existing methods drops when trained on our augmented, column-agnostic dataset, and that our own method reaches state of the art accuracy, while relying on column contents only.

1 Introduction

Recent developments in Natural Language Understanding (NLU) have led to a big proliferation of text- and speech-based bot interfaces. Home appliances, such as smart speakers and chatbots, rely mostly on a well-structured knowledge base or an external Application Programming Interface (API) to provide the desired response. This limits the usability of such systems in a context where the data is stored in a (local) relational database.

This constraint led to the development of text to Structured Query Language (SQL) systems, also known as SQL bots. Given a question, in natural language, pertaining to a certain database table, these bots will automatically generate the corresponding SQL query and return the requested data. Considering the vast usage of relational databases on the internet and in private companies, SQL bots are a simple new interface that enables nontechnical people to access data.

The first approaches in the field relied on parsers and pattern-matching rules to understand the question and produce appropriate answers (Androutsopoulos et al., 1995). Later developments introduced semantic grammar systems and intermediate language systems (Androutsopoulos et al., 1995). More recently, new NLU methods, such as pointer-networks, pushed the state-of-the-art results in several domains, including parsing (Vinyals et al., 2015). Current state-of-the-art models are based on sketches and have primarily two inputs: the question and the descriptions of the table columns (i.e., the column names).

Relying on the column names is limiting, since the whole model is based on several strong premises: (a) the names are high quality and descriptive enough; (b) the names do not change; (c) the names are known to the user of the bot. These are very strong assumptions: often, column names do not even exist (i.e., the generic col1, col2, etc. are used instead). Moreover, if as we observe in Figure 1, a column contains the names of colleges, just changing the column name form "College" to "School" does not make the content any less informative. The expectation from a bot is that their quality is not sensitive to cosmetic changes to the underlying table. Finally, users do not necessarily know the structure of the table, let alone the column names.

In this paper, we build and present ICE (Individual Column Embeddings) – a novel approach of representing the database table columns, by using their contents instead of their names. To do so,

---

[1]equal contribution

Proceedings of the 2018 EMNLP Workshop SCAI: The 2nd Int'l Workshop on Search-Oriented Conversational AI, pages 67–73
Brussels, Belgium, October 31, 2018. ©2018 Association for Computational Linguistics

Attribute

pick	CFL Team	Player	Position	College
27	Hamilton Tiger-Cats	Connor Healy	DB	Wilfrid Laurier
28	Calgary Stampeders	Anthony Forgone	OL	York
29	Ottawa Renegades	L.P. Ladouceur	DT	California
27	Toronto Argonauts	Frank Hoffman	DL	York

Figure 1: Part of a table from the WikiSQL dataset with the contexts within a relation (table) we can model

we construct a column embedding vector space, where we embed the columns. This embedding is then used as a substitute for the encoding of the column descriptions (headers) in a state of the art sketch-based model.

In addition, to empirically show the value of using ICE, we generate a new, column-agnostic dataset based on the widely used WikiSQL dataset (Zhong et al., 2017). In WikiSQL, a substantial bias towards the inclusion in the question of the column name is built-in. For instance more than 79% of questions contain the name of the column that needs to be selected. Additionally around 59% contain the names of all columns form the SQL `where` clause. With ICE, we are eliminating the strong assumption that the users have access to the table structure. Hence, we also need a less biased dataset to show the value of our method.

We thus create an open source data augmentation tool to paraphrase part of the questions in WikiSQL: where the column names are present, we replace them with similar expressions (e.g., synonyms), removing some of the built-in bias.

We train and test our ICE-based model on both the original WikiSQL dataset and our column-agnostic version of the dataset. We show that we maintain the same accuracy on both datasets with all three tasks: aggregation, column-selection and *where* clause generation. We also train the original SQLNet (Zhong et al., 2017) model on the column-agnostic dataset and find a 7% accuracy drop in the *where* clause generation task.

In a nutshell, the most important contribution of this work is that we **improve the model resilience** by limiting its reliance on arbitrary descriptions of the data within the tables. In addition, we **expand the applicability of SQL bots** to users who do not know the internal structure of the databases they are trying to access. By eliminating the need to encode the column headers, we also **reduce the overall complexity of the model**. This is achieved by removing the LSTM networks used to generate unique column header encodings

for the aggregation prediction, selection prediction and *where* clause generation.

The paper is organized as follows: Section 2 presents the related work for translating sentences to SQL and for vector space embeddings. In Section 3, we describe ICE – our method for column content embeddings. In the next section, we introduce our column-agnostic model for translating sentences to SQL. We present the evaluation results in Section 5 and finally conclude in Section 6.

2 Related Work

2.1 Related work in Sentences to SQL

Systems that enable users to use natural language to interact with a database have been researched since the early seventies. As summarized in (Androutsopoulos et al., 1995) these early approaches were mostly rule-based. More successful methods have emerged since the advent of the sequence to sequence (Sutskever et al., 2014) neural network architectures and increased availability of training data in recent years. The first model to leverage this was SEQ2SQL introduced by (Zhong et al., 2017) together with their crowdsourced dataset WikiSQL. SEQ2SQL solves the problem of generating SQL queries in a three-step approach that aligns with the structure of an SQL query. First, it determines the aggregation function for the query i.e. whether to apply count, average, max etc. This is performed by a classifier trained on the encoding of the question and the encodings of the table headers. In the second step, the model determines the column on which to perform the selection, again based on the encoding of the question and the encodings of the table headers. Finally, in the last step, the model generates the where clause of the SQL query. To do so it first determines the number of conditions in the clause and then proceeds to generate tuples of a column, comparison operator and value using a pointer network. Since the order in the where clause is not important when there are multiple conditions the model also im-

68

plements a reinforcement learning policy to optimize for execution correctness and uses a mixed loss function.

SQLNet (Xu et al., 2017) improved upon SEQ2SQL by eliminating the need for reinforcement learning by using a sketch-based approach. (Bornholt et al., 2016; Solar-Lezama et al., 2006) In the where clause section SQLNet introduces a sequence-to-set model. It first picks a set of columns which will be used in the clause. Subsequently, for each column, it determines a comparison operator using a classifier and picks a comparison value using a printer network. Additionally, this model implements a column attention mechanism which together with sequence-to-set model improves the accuracy over SEQ2SQL by 9% to 13%.

2.2 From Word to Table Embeddings

The most basic form of word embeddings is the bag of words model. It can be augmented by statistics such as TF-IDF, however, such vector space captures very little of the words semantics, morphology, hierarchy and context. Word2vec, introduced by (Mikolov et al., 2013) is one of the first popular neural embedding models. It comes in two general implementations: a continuous bag of words (order in window irrelevant) and a continuous skip gram (weight in window based on distance from current word). The objective function of Word2vec causes words that appear in a similar context to cluster together in the vector space, based on cosine distance. This method was modified by the introduction of global word representation which aims to capture the meaning of the word within the whole corpus (Pennington et al., 2014) and the use of subword information to capture the morphology of the words (Joulin et al., 2016).

With the addition of simple techniques, such as a trained weighted average, word-embedding algorithms were further extended to embed whole sentences (Pagliardini et al., 2018) and whole documents (Le and Mikolov, 2014). Such techniques have also recently been used to get the embedding of whole tables for the purposes of table classification (Ghasemi-Gol and Szekely, 2018).

3 ICE: Individual Column Embeddings

To understand the context and the hierarchy of a table we will use the formal definition of a rela-

tion: "a set of tuples $(d_1, d_2, ..., d_n)$, where each element d_j is a member of D_j, the $j - th$ data domain." Tuples, relations and attributes are graphically depicted in Figure 1. We observe that there are two contexts in which an element, or cell, d_j appers either within a tuple (row) or within a data domain (column).

To embed the whole table we need to look at both contexts. This complexity is not necessary in the context of individual column embeddings, where the latter context is sufficient. TabVec uses deviation from the median for table vectors to capture the noise (Ghasemi-Gol and Szekely, 2018), as the final table vector incorporates information from cells that are not conceptually similar. This is not the case for individual column embeddings, as for ICE we assume that the cells within a column are conceptually similar. For instance, if the column is about locations, all the cells are likely to represent location names. This property allows us to simplify the aggregation and use the median vector of all cells as the column representation.

Table cells are not semantic atoms and can contain multiple words, for example in Figure 1 all *Team* names contain at least two words. Thus, given a vector space model for words, we compute the individual cell embedding (ICE) as the average of the word embeddings and the individual column embedding as the median of its cells.

To sum up, let a column D contain cells $c_i \in C(D)$, with each cell consisting of a sequence of n_i words $(w_{i1}, ..., w_{ij}, ..., w_{in_i})$. Given a function E that computes a word embedding, the ICE of the D is defined as:

$$E(D) = median_{c_i}(\frac{1}{n_i} \sum_{j=0}^{n_i} E(w_{ij})), c_i \in C(D)$$

3.1 Table Word Embeddings.

For the ICE to be meaningful, the word embeddings need to reflect the table semantics. The way words are used in tables differs significantly from the way they appear in normal language. We keep the intuition that a word can be represented as an aggretation over all the contexts in which that word appears. What changes from typical text embeddings (Mikolov et al., 2013; Pennington et al., 2014) is that the context is given by other words that occur in the same table column. We view column tables as synthetic sentences that allow us to learn what the relevant context is. We then use

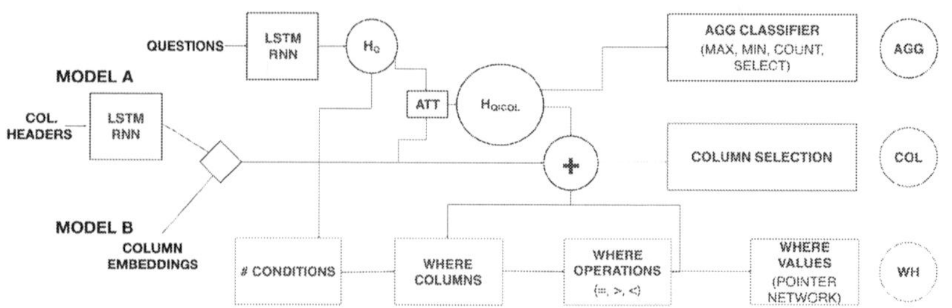

Figure 2: The general network architecture of SQLNet. Model A represents the original model, while Model B represents our model.

SkipGrams with a window of 5 to generate the embedding model.

We first construct a data corpus of synthetic sentences, corresponding to columns. We define a sentence as all the cells in one table column concatenated. Furthermore, we make the assumption that the order of the cells within a column is not important. For the table in Figure 1, a sample sentence would be *Calgary Stampeders Ottawa Renegades Toronto Argonauts Hamilton Tiger-Cats*. We generate 10 random cell shuffles of each column. Using this corpus we train a word2vec model with the Gensim toolkit (Řehůřek and Sojka, 2010).

4 Individual Column Embedding for Bot Resilience

Our work builds upon the SQLNet (Xu et al., 2017) sketch-based approach. To generate a SQL statement, each component of the query is generated individually: *the aggregation*, the *column selection* and the *where clauses*. The task is thus akin to slot filling (Xu et al., 2017). The process is graphically depicted in Figure 2. The input or the SQLNet and previous models (Xu et al., 2017) consists of a representation of the question and a representation of each table column header.

We believe this assumption represents one of the most important drawbacks of the approach, as knowledge about the column headers may not exist in real world conditions. The reason this knowledge was used in previous work is that the dataset itself was biased towards explicitly including the column names in the question formulation. In this section we show how to build a dataset that alleviates this bias. We then use the new dataset to create a model that relies on the column content , not on the column headers.

Column type	Train	Test	Dev
Selection col.	79.0%	79.0%	79.65%
Where col. >= 1	68.0%	67.6%	68.4%
All where col.	58.9%	58.5%	59.2%

Table 1: The percentages in the table show the proportion of questions that contain the specific column header in the different data partitions.

4.1 Column-agnostic WikiSQL

The wikiSQL dataset was crowdsourced using tables from Wikipedia. Workers on Amazon Mechanical Turk[1] were presented with a table and a generated SQL query and were asked to ask a question that matched the query. This method introduces an inherent bias in the dataset as demonstrated in Table 1. Almost 80% of questions contain the column name that is retrieved in the selection step and 68% of questions contain at least one of the column names from the where clause. In total, only 11% of the questions do not contain **exact matches** of the column names, as shown in Figure 1. As the workers were shown the whole table with column names, in a large number of cases they copied the column name in the question.

We paraphrase questions that contain a column name to make the dataset more realistic, as described in Algorithm 1. We create candidate questions by replacing the names with synonyms that share the syntactic and semantic properties of the original names.

The original question and the candidate questions are then embedded in vector space with sent2vec (Pagliardini et al., 2018). Using these vector space representations we compute the cosine similarity between the original question and

---

[1] https://www.mturk.com/

the potential replacements and choose the most similar candidate. This procedure yields a suitable rephrasing for 20% of the dataset, as we did not find synonyms for all questions containing column names. For instance, the orginal questions *What is the length (miles) of endpoints westlake/macarthur park to wilshire/western?*, which contains the column header **length (miles)**, becomes *What is the distance (miles) of endpoints westlake/macarthur park to wilshire/western?*.

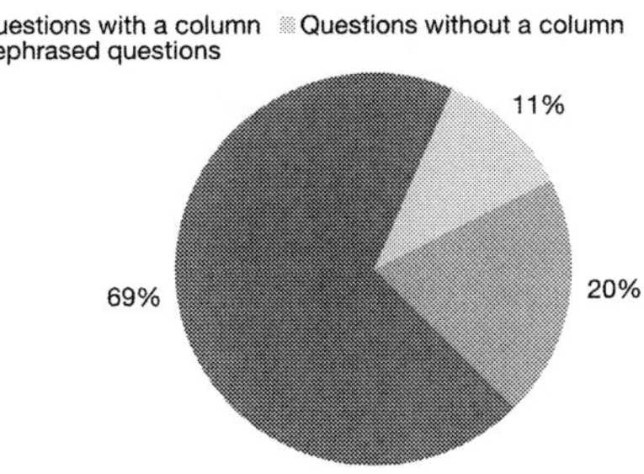

Figure 3: Proportions of the modified dataset

Data: Question and column header
Result: Replacement candidate questions
Tokenize and pos tag question;
for *word in column header* **do**
  Get word tag in question;
  Get word synonyms using tag;
  if *synonyms list > 0* **then**
    append synonyms to rephrase list;
  end
end
for *phrase in rephrase list* **do**
  if *length of phrase == length of header*
  then
    replace column header in question
      with phrase;
    append new question to candidate list;
  end
end
Algorithm 1: Generating replacement candidate questions

4.2 Integrating Individual Column Embeddings

We compute the embeddings for the entire table column corpus as described in chapter 3. This is necessary since the embeddings are required during inference both during training and testing. Due to model size constraints, we keep the individual column embeddings constant during both training and testing. We create a dictionary to link each column to its embedding vector and feed it to the model (Model B) in Figure 2. An attention mechanism has the embeddings as inputs and the result contributes to the aggregation, selection and where clause modules. The column vectors are generated with the same dimensions that we use for the question encoding.

As we replace the column headers with column content embeddings, our model is completely agnostic to the headers. We thus remove the LSTM used to encode the column headers in the three model components: aggregation, selection and where clause generation. This leads to a significant **reduction in the complexity of the model**.

5 Evaluation

5.1 Original WikiSQL Evaluation

The evaluation on the full original WikiSQL dataset determines whether the individual column embeddings are suitable replacements for headers when the column name appears in the question. Table 2 summarizes the results of our model *SQLNet+ICE* and compares them with the results of two baselines: *SQLNet* and *Seq2SQL*. We portray the accuracy values on the development and test sets for the three slots we fill in the sketch: *Aggregation function*, *Column Selection* and *Where clause generation*.

We observe that *SQLNet+ICE* performs similarly to the original *SQLNet* model in both cases and superior to *Seq2SQL*. This result shows that we can build an equally performing model that is resilient to changes to the DB schema or complete absence of knowledge about it.

We note that the accuracy of the aggregation function also changes. This happens because the aggregation classifier has either the column or header embeddings as inputs, as shown in 2. There is a small decrease of accuracy for the Aggregation and Where clauses, while the accuracy on the Column Selection performs slightly better. These results are expected, as the queries strongly rely on the direct column names mentions.

5.2 Column-agnostic WikiSQL Evaluation

The second experiment shows the more realistic results, obtained on the column-agnostic WikiSQL Dataset. The results in Table 3 show that SQLNet struggles to predict correctly the column related

	Dev Set Accuracy			Test Set Accuracy		
	Aggregation	Selection	Where-clause	Aggregation	Selection	Where-clause
Seq2SQL	90.0%	89.6%	62.1%	90.1%	88.9%	60.2%
SQLNet	90.1%	91.5%	74.1%	90.3%	90.9%	71.9%
SQLNet + ICE	89.7 %	92.4	72.2%	89.3 %	91.8	71.1%

Table 2: Model accuracies on the Original WikiSQL Dataset

	Dev Set Accuracy			Test Set Accuracy		
	Aggregation	Selection	Where-clause	Aggregation	Selection	Where-clause
SQLNet	90.1%	87.5%	63.4%	90.3%	87.1%	63.1%
SQLNet + ICE	89.7 %	88.4	70.1%	89.3 %	87.9	69.4%

Table 3: Model accuracies on the Column-agnostic WikiSQL Dataset

	Rephrased Test Set Accuracy		
	Agg.	Sel.	W.-clause
SQLNet	89.5 %	81.3%	43.2%
SQLNet + ICE	88.9 %	83.2	61.3%

Table 4: Model accuracies on the paraphrased questions only on Aggreation, Selection and Where-clause tasks.

parts of the query, especially in the case of the where clause generation. This drop in the accuracy is expected, since the where clause predictor is the most complex part of the model. Without the original dataset bias where the column names were present in the questions, the column names are not descriptive enough.This leads to a drop of 10.7% on the validation and 8.8% on test dataset.

On the other hand, our model is capable of overcoming this situation and find the queries with a much smaller drop of accuracy. Although the performance is also worse than with the original dataset, the accuracy obtained using SQLNet with individual column embeddings in the where clauses is only 2.1% lower in validation and 1.7% in test. Using individual column embeddings makes the SQLNet model more versatile, as it can address the scenario where the user is not aware of the table structure.

Focusing on rephrased questions. To better understand our results on the Column-agnostic WikiSQL dataset we run the evaluation just with questions that have been rephrased, which represent around 20% of the whole data set, as shown in Figure 3. Table 4 summarizes these results, with SQLNet is the original model described in (Xu et al., 2017). The previously seen drop in *SQLNet* accuracy on the column selection and where-clause predictions is exacerbated - showing that indeed the paraphrasing is indeed the root cause. This effect is comparatively mild in *SQLNet + ICE*.

6 Conclusion and Future Work

In this paper, we proposed a new approach to build SQL chatbots without relying on the database table schema. Previous work built around the WikiSQL dataset take advantage of the dataset biases and use the column names to improve performance. This reliance on the schema inhibits their generalization capacity to cases where schema knowledge is absent. Our model, built on SQLNet by adding Individual Column Embeddings *SQLNet + ICE*, does not suffer from these limitations.

We provide a way to create Individual Column Embeddings, different from the Column Embeddings in prior art (Ghasemi-Gol and Szekely, 2018). Furthermore, we publish a method to paraphrase WikiSQL questions to alleviate the dataset bias.

The results of our model on the paraphrased WikiSQL are very similar to the ones obtained on the original dataset, while the SQLNet models struggles to deal with the paraphrasing.

Future Work. Even with these changes, there is still room for improvement in the SQL chatbot area. Large scale operations need the support for multiple tables at the time as well as more operations such as *join*. While WikiSQL is a good starting point and our modified version removes some of the biases present in it, there is a strong need for more data, both in terms of quantity and diversity. This new data needs to include more operations, as well as new ways to collect questions to have more variety in the structure of the user's utterances.

References

Ion Androutsopoulos, Graeme D. Ritchie, and Peter Thanisch. 1995. Natural language interfaces to databases - an introduction. *CoRR*, cmp-lg/9503016.

James Bornholt, Emina Torlak, Dan Grossman, and Luis Ceze. 2016. Optimizing synthesis with metasketches. In *Proceedings of the 43rd Annual ACM SIGPLAN-SIGACT Symposium on Principles of Programming Languages*, POPL '16, pages 775–788, New York, NY, USA. ACM.

Majid Ghasemi-Gol and Pedro A. Szekely. 2018. Tabvec: Table vectors for classification of web tables. *CoRR*, abs/1802.06290.

Armand Joulin, Edouard Grave, Piotr Bojanowski, and Tomas Mikolov. 2016. Bag of tricks for efficient text classification. *CoRR*, abs/1607.01759.

Quoc V. Le and Tomas Mikolov. 2014. Distributed representations of sentences and documents. *CoRR*, abs/1405.4053.

Tomas Mikolov, Ilya Sutskever, Kai Chen, Greg S Corrado, and Jeff Dean. 2013. Distributed representations of words and phrases and their compositionality. In C. J. C. Burges, L. Bottou, M. Welling, Z. Ghahramani, and K. Q. Weinberger, editors, *Advances in Neural Information Processing Systems 26*, pages 3111–3119. Curran Associates, Inc.

Matteo Pagliardini, Prakhar Gupta, and Martin Jaggi. 2018. Unsupervised Learning of Sentence Embeddings using Compositional n-Gram Features. In *NAACL 2018 - Conference of the North American Chapter of the Association for Computational Linguistics*.

Jeffrey Pennington, Richard Socher, and Christopher D. Manning. 2014. Glove: Global vectors for word representation. In *In EMNLP*.

Radim Řehůřek and Petr Sojka. 2010. Software Framework for Topic Modelling with Large Corpora. In *Proceedings of the LREC 2010 Workshop on New Challenges for NLP Frameworks*, pages 45–50, Valletta, Malta. ELRA. `http://is.muni.cz/publication/884893/en`.

Armando Solar-Lezama, Liviu Tancau, Rastislav Bodik, Sanjit Seshia, and Vijay Saraswat. 2006. Combinatorial sketching for finite programs. *SIGPLAN Not.*, 41(11):404–415.

Ilya Sutskever, Oriol Vinyals, and Quoc V. Le. 2014. Sequence to sequence learning with neural networks. *CoRR*, abs/1409.3215.

Oriol Vinyals, Meire Fortunato, and Navdeep Jaitly. 2015. Pointer networks. In C. Cortes, N. D. Lawrence, D. D. Lee, M. Sugiyama, and R. Garnett, editors, *Advances in Neural Information Processing Systems 28*, pages 2692–2700. Curran Associates, Inc.

Xiaojun Xu, Chang Liu, and Dawn Song. 2017. Sqlnet: Generating structured queries from natural language without reinforcement learning. *CoRR*, abs/1711.04436.

Victor Zhong, Caiming Xiong, and Richard Socher. 2017. Seq2sql: Generating structured queries from natural language using reinforcement learning. *CoRR*, abs/1709.00103.

Exploring Named Entity Recognition As an Auxiliary Task for Slot Filling in Conversational Language Understanding

Samuel Louvan
University of Trento
Fondazione Bruno Kessler
slouvan@fbk.eu

Bernardo Magnini
Fondazione Bruno Kessler
magnini@fbk.eu

Abstract

Slot filling is a crucial task in the Natural Language Understanding (NLU) component of a dialogue system. Most approaches for this task rely solely on the domain-specific datasets for training. We propose a joint model of slot filling and Named Entity Recognition (NER) in a multi-task learning (MTL) setup. Our experiments on three slot filling datasets show that using NER as an auxiliary task improves slot filling performance and achieve competitive performance compared with state-of-the-art. In particular, NER is effective when supervised at the lower layer of the model. For low-resource scenarios, we found that MTL is effective for one dataset.

1 Introduction

Most of the current dialogue systems depend on an NLU component to extract semantic information from an utterance. Such semantic information is often represented as a semantic frame which contains the domain, intent of the user, and predefined attributes (*slots*). Each word of the utterance is labeled with a slot, which defines a particular attribute (an entity, time, etc) of the utterance. Table 1 shows an example of a semantic frame for the sentence *"Show me the prices of all flights from Atlanta to Washington DC"* with Begin/In/Out (BIO) representation.

We focus on *slot filling*, a task of automatically extracting slots for a given utterance. This task can be treated as a sequence labeling problem and the most successful approach is to employ a conditional random fields (CRF) on top of a deep recurrent neural networks (RNN). In general, there are two ways of training a slot filling model: (i) train a domain-specific model (Goo et al., 2018; Wang et al., 2018) or (ii) train a model that performs well across domains using domain adaptation or transfer learning techniques (Hakkani-Tür

| Domain | airline |
| **Intent** | search airfare |

Utterance	Slot Label
show	O
me	O
the	O
prices	O
of	O
all	O
flights	O
from	O
Atlanta	B-fromloc.city_name
to	O
Washington	B-toloc.city_name
DC	I-toloc.city_name

Table 1: An example of a semantic frame with its coressponding domain, intent and slots.

et al., 2016; Jaech et al., 2016; Jha et al., 2018; Kim et al., 2017). One popular transfer learning technique is multi-task learning (MTL) (Caruana, 1997) in which a joint model is trained on a target (main) task and several auxiliary tasks simultaneously to learn better feature representations across tasks. This technique has shown potential on various NLP tasks and offer flexibility as it allows transfer learning across different domains and tasks (Yang et al., 2017). On slot filling, Jaech et al. (2016) train a single slot filling model on different domains and show that MTL is particulary useful in low resource scenarios.

Identifying beneficial auxiliary task for the target task is important when applying MTL (Bingel and Søgaard, 2017). In this work, we investigate the effectiveness of Named Entity Recognition (NER) as an auxiliary task for slot filling. We propose NER because of two main reasons. First, the slot values are typically named entities, for example airline name, city name, etc. Second, the state of the art performance of models for NER have been relatively high (Lample et al., 2016; Ma and Hovy, 2016). Therefore, we expect that the

Proceedings of the 2018 EMNLP Workshop SCAI: The 2nd Int'l Workshop on Search-Oriented Conversational AI, pages 74–80
Brussels, Belgium, October 31, 2018. ©2018 Association for Computational Linguistics

learned features of NER can improve the slot filling performance. Finally, NER corpus is relatively easier to obtain compared to domain specific slot filling datasets.

We are interested to answer the following questions:

- *Does NER help the performance of slot filling in the MTL setup?* As NER labels are usually more coarse-grained than slot filling labels, predicted NER label might provide good signal to the more fine-grained slot labels. For example, the location `LOC` label in NER can be a strong indicator for slots `fromloc.city_name` or `toloc.city_name` and filter out other slot labels which are not related to location. We hope the model can learn more general knowledge first and transfer such knowledge to predict more specific slot information using MTL.

- *What is the effect of supervising NER on the lower layer of the MTL model to the slot filling performance?* Inspired by recent work of Søgaard and Goldberg (2016), we investigate the effect of supervising NER on different layers of the model. Our hypothesis is that a more "general" feature is better learned on the lower layer in order to support a task which depends on a more "specific" feature.

In addition, we also experiment on cross-domain slot filling models by jointly training slot filling datasets from *similar* domains using a MTL setup. We explore two techniques to measure similarity between domains: domain similarity by Ruder and Plank (2017a) and label embedding mapping by Kim et al. (2015).

We experiment with three datasets from different domains. Our experiments show that for all datasets, using NER as an auxiliary task is beneficial for the slot filling performance. NER is consistently helpful when it is supervised at the lower layer. On the low resource scenario, we found mixed results, in which MTL is only effective for 1 dataset.

2 Model

This section describes the slot filling model, the multi-task learning setup, and the data selection that we use in our experiments.

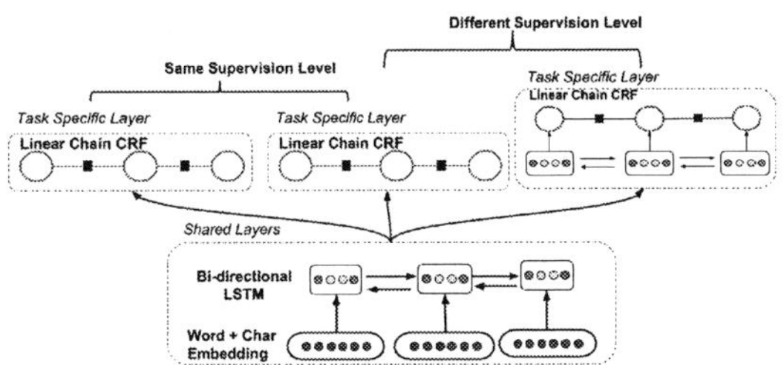

Figure 1: Multi-task Learning with different supervision level

2.1 Slot Filling Model

For the slot filling model, we adopt a neural based model similar to (Lample et al., 2016; Ma and Hovy, 2016), as it achieves the state of the art performance in sequence labeling task (NER). Recent slot filling model of Jha et al. (2018) also used a variant of this model. Given an input sentence, we represent each word w_i using a concatenation of its word embedding $\mathbf{e}(w_i)$ and character-level embeddings $\mathbf{c}(w_i)$: $\mathbf{x}_i = [\mathbf{e}(w_i); \mathbf{c}(w_i)]$. The character-level embeddings are computed using convolutional neural networks (CNN), similar to the one proposed by Kim et al. (2016). We then feed $\mathbf{x}_i$ to a bidirectional LSTM (biLSTM) word-level encoder to incorporate the contextual information of w_i. The output of the backward and forward LSTM at each time step is then concatenated and fed into a CRF layer. The CRF layer computes the final output, e.g. the tag of each input. We use one hidden layer between biLSTM and CRF as it has been shown by Lample et al. (2016) that it can improve performance.

2.2 Multi-Task Learning

One simple technique to perform MTL is by training the target and auxiliary tasks simultaneously. In this setting, the parameters of the model are shared across tasks, pushing the model to learn feature representations that work well across tasks.

Figure 1 depicts the MTL setting that we use in our work. The lower parts of the network, i.e. word embeddings, character-level embeddings, and bi-LSTM encoder are shared among tasks. After the bi-LSTM layer, we use different CRF layers for each task to predict the task-specific tags (NER or slot filling). We also experiment with MTL setup which uses different level of supervision for the auxiliary task (Søgaard and Goldberg, 2016), in which we use two layers of biLSTM encoder and only share the lower layer of

Dataset	#sent			#token	#label	Label Examples
	train	dev	test			
Slot Filling						
ATIS	4478	500	893	869	79	airport name, airline name, return date
MIT Restaurant	6128	1532	3385	4166	8	restaurant name, dish, price, hours
MIT Movie	7820	1955	2443	5953	12	actor, director, genre, title, character
NER						
CoNLL 2003	14987	3466	3684	21010	4	person, location, organization
OntoNotes 5.0	34970	5896	2327	34662	18	organization, gpe, date, money, quantity

Table 2: Statistics of the datasets. For each dataset, number of sentence in train/dev/test set, the number of unique token and label in the training set.

the encoder and keep the outer layer for the main slot filling task.

2.3 Data Selection

Ruder and Plank (2017b) demonstrate that selecting data for training the auxiliary task might improve the target task performance. We investigate two data selection techniques for our MTL experiments:

Domain Similarity. We use Jensen-Shannon divergence (JSD; Lin, 1991) to measure domain similarity as proposed by Ruder and Plank (2017b): $\frac{1}{2}(D_{KL}(P||M) + D_{KL}(K||M))$ where $M = \frac{1}{2}(P + Q)$. $D_{KL}(P||Q)$ is the Kullback-Leibler divergence between two distributions P and Q. We use term distributions (Plank and Van Noord, 2011) of each domain to compute P and Q. We select the most similar domain to the main task domain to be used as the *auxiliary task*.

Label Embedding Mapping. In an MTL setup, sometimes we only want to keep auxiliary labels which are semantically similar to target task labels and remove other irrelevant labels of the auxiliary task. For example, the slot filling label `airport.statename` is similar to `LOC` but not to `TIME` auxiliary NER label. We employ label embedding mapping approach by Kim et al. (2015) using Canonical Correlation Analysis (CCA). The idea is to construct matrix representation where rows are labels and columns are words in the vocabulary. The cell value in the matrix is the pointwise mutual information (PMI) between the label and the word. After that, we perform rank-k SVD on the matrix and normalized the rows of the matrix. Each row with k dimension of the matrix is the label embedding of a particular label. We use the cosine similarity between two label embedding representations to obtain the nearest neighbor.

Target Task	Most Similar Domain
ATIS	MIT-R
MIT-R	MIT-M
MIT-M	MIT-R

Table 3: Most similar domain for each target task computed with JSD

3 Experimental Setup

Data. We use three slot filling datasets (Table 2): Airline Travel Information System (ATIS; Tür et al., 2010), MIT Restaurant (MIT-R) and MIT Movie (MIT-M) (Liu et al., 2013; Liu and Lane, 2017b). The ATIS dataset is widely used in conversational language understanding and contains queries to a flight database. We use the provided slot annotations and use the same split as in Hakkani-Tür et al. (2016). The MIT-R contains utterances related to restaurant search and MIT-M contains queries related to movie information. For both datasets, we use the default split.[1] As for the NER dataset, we use two datasets : CoNLL 2003 (Tjong Kim Sang and De Meulder, 2003) and Ontonotes 5.0 (Pradhan et al., 2013). For OntoNotes, we use the Newswire section for our experiments.

Implementation. We use the existing BiLSTM-CRF sequence tagger implementation from Reimers and Gurevych (2017) for all experiments.[2] We use the pre-trained word embedding from (Komninos and Manandhar, 2016). We set the LSTM hidden units to 100. The word and character embeddings dimensions are set to 300 and 30 respectively. We use dropout rate of 0.25. We train the model using the Adam optimizer (Kingma and Ba, 2014) for 25 epochs with early stopping on the target task. For each epoch, we

---

[1] https://groups.csail.mit.edu/sls/downloads/
[2] https://github.com/UKPLab/emnlp2017-bilstm-cnn-crf

Model	Aux. Task		Target Task		
	SF	NER	ATIS	MIT-R	MIT-M
Bi-model based (Wang et al., 2018)	-	-	**96.89**	-	-
Slot gated model (Goo et al., 2018)	-	-	95.20	-	-
Recurrent Attention (Liu and Lane, 2016)	-	-	95.87	-	-
Adversarial(Liu and Lane, 2017a)	-	-	95.63	74.47	85.33
Single task (STL)	-	-	95.68	78.58	<u>87.34</u>
MTL, same supervision level	most similar	-	95.47	78.56	86.89
MTL, same supervision level	all	-	95.68	78.70	87.22
MTL, same supervision level	most similar	✓	95.50	78.41	86.77
MTL, same supervision level	all	✓	95.34	78.27	86.76
MTL, same supervision level	-	✓	95.71	78.40	87.09
MTL, different supervision level	most similar	✓	95.70	<u>79.10</u>	86.94
MTL, different supervision level	all	✓	<u>95.94</u>	79.00	86.92
MTL, different supervision level	-	✓	95.40	**79.13**	**87.41**

Table 4: F1 scores comparison between MTL, STL, and previous published results on each dataset. "Most Similar" auxiliary task means we take the most similar slot filling domain (excluding NER) as the auxiliary task. "All" includes all the slot filling domains as the auxiliary tasks (excluding NER). For the "different supervision level", NER is supervised at the lower layer and slot filling tasks at the higher layer. Bold: best, Underline: second best.

train the model of each task in alternate fashion. We evaluate the performance by computing the F1-score on the test set using the standard CoNLL-2000 evaluation[3]

Target Task & Auxiliary Tasks. For each MTL experiment, there is exactly one target task and one or more auxiliary task(s). The target task is always a slot filling task, i.e. either ATIS, MIT-R, or MIT-M. The auxiliary task(s) consist of a combination of slot filling tasks from different domains of the target task with (or without) a NER task. We select the most similar slot filling task for the target task using the domain similarity technique described in (§2.3). Table 3 presents the most similar slot filling domain for each slot filling task.

4 Results and Analysis

Overall Performance. Table 4 summarizes the slot filling performance of our single task (STL) versus MTL models. The performance from previous studies are directly copied from their reported numbers. When using the same supervision level for both target and auxiliary tasks, using the most similar domain performs worse than using all domains. In contrast, using NER together with the most similar domain as auxiliary tasks performs better than using all the domains.

Experiments on different supervision level show that using NER as an auxiliary task consistently improves slot filling performance. This re-

sult matches our intuition that the task with more coarse-label, such as NER, is better to be supervised at the lower layer of the model. On ATIS and MIT-R datasets, MTL achieves better performance compared to STL. However, on MIT-M, STL outperforms some MTL models.

In order to understand better the behavior of the models, we analyze the results from the development set. For the ATIS dataset, STL and MTL have the same performance in 44 out of 67 slots in the development set. For the rest of the slots, STL performs better mostly on slots related to time such as `arrive_time.time` and `depart_date.month_name` while MTL is better on recognizing location related slots such as `city_name` and `toloc.state_name`. For the MIT Restaurant dataset, MTL performs better on 5 out of 8 slots. MTL performs well in identifying slots related to time and location in the MIT Restaurant dataset. For the MIT movie, MTL yields better results for time related slots. As for the person related slots such as `character`, `actor`, and `director`, STL gives better results. Overall, although incorporating NER with slot filling shows improvements, the difference is still rather small especially for the ATIS and the MIT Movie datasets. Further work is needed to explore better mechanism to inject NER information to help slot filling in the MTL setup. It is also interesting to compare the performance of MTL and pipeline based system which utilizes NER prediction as one of the feature for the slot filling model.

---

[3]https://www.clips.uantwerpen.be/conll2000/chunking/output.htm

Model	ATIS	MIT-R	MIT-M
MTL	**95.94**	**79.10**	**87.34**
MTL+Label Emb.	95.66	78.37	86.84

Table 5: The effect of the label filtering on MTL performance

Dataset	# training sents	STL	MTL
ATIS	200	**83.88**	81.27
	400	**85.54**	85.21
	800	90.48	**90.68**
MIT-R	200	54.65	**54.91**
	400	61.36	**61.88**
	800	67.48	**68.27**
MIT-M	200	68.28	**69.12**
	400	74.09	**75.15**[††]
	800	**79.33**	79.08

Table 6: Performance comparison between STL and MTL for low resource scenarios. †† indicates significant improvement over STL baseline with $p < 0.05$ using approximate randomization testing.

Effect of Label Embedding Mapping. We apply label filtering on the auxiliary tasks using the label embedding mapping (§2.3). On the auxiliary dataset(s), we keep the most similar labels and replace irrelevant labels with O. The MTL setup that we use is the best performing MTL for each dataset in Table 4. As shown in Table 5, the performance of MTL drops when we apply filtering to the auxiliary labels. We suspect that this is due to the quality of the label mapping and also a high number of "O" label after the filtering process.

Low Resource Scenarios. We experiment on low resource scenarios where we vary the number of training sentences to 200, 400, and 800 sentences for each dataset. The MTL setup that we use is the best performing MTL for each dataset in Table 4. As shown in Table 6, MTL consistently performs better than STL for the MIT-R dataset. While for the ATIS and MIT-M datasets, STL mostly gives better results than MTL.

5 Related Work

Recent studies on slot filling in conversational systems are mostly based on neural models. Wang et al. (2018) introduce a bi-model (RNN) structure to consider cross-impact between intent detection and slot filling. Liu and Lane (2016) propose an attention mechanism on the encoder-decoder model for joint intent classification and slot filling. (Goo et al., 2018) extend the attention mechanism us-

ing a slot gated model to learn relationship between slot and intent attention vectors. Hakkani-Tür et al. (2016) use bidirectional RNN as a single model that handle multiple domains by adding a final state that contains domain identifier. The work by Jha et al. (2018); Kim et al. (2017) uses expert based domain adaptation while Jaech et al. (2016) propose a multi-task learning approach to guide the training of a model for new domain. All of these studies train their model solely on slot filling datasets, while our focus is to exploit a more "general" resource, such as NER, by training the model jointly with slot filling through MTL with different supervision level.

6 Conclusion

In this work, we investigate the effectiveness of training a slot filling model jointly with NER as an auxiliary task through MTL setup. Our experiments demonstrate that NER is helpful for slot filling. In particular, NER is more effective when it is supervised at the lower layer of the MTL model. However, further work is needed to investigate the effectiveness of domain similarity metric or label embedding mapping as a way to perform data selection in the preprocessing step.

Acknowledgments

The authors would like to thank anonymous reviewers and Clara Vania for the helpful comments and feedback. This work was supported by the grant of Fondazione Bruno Kessler PhD scholarship.

References

Joachim Bingel and Anders Søgaard. 2017. Identifying beneficial task relations for multi-task learning in deep neural networks. *EACL 2017*, page 164.

Rich Caruana. 1997. Multitask learning. *Machine Learning*, 28:41–75.

Chih-Wen Goo, Guang Gao, Yun-Kai Hsu, Chih-Li Huo, Tsung-Chieh Chen, Keng-Wei Hsu, and Yun-Nung Chen. 2018. Slot-gated modeling for joint slot filling and intent prediction. In *Proceedings of the 2018 Conference of the North American Chapter of the Association for Computational Linguistics: Human Language Technologies, NAACL-HLT, New Orleans, Louisiana, USA, June 1-6, 2018, Volume 2 (Short Papers)*, pages 753–757.

Dilek Z. Hakkani-Tür, Gökhan Tür, Asli elikyilmaz, Yun-Nung Chen, Jianfeng Gao, Li Deng, and Ye-Yi Wang. 2016. Multi-domain joint semantic frame parsing using bi-directional rnn-lstm. In *INTER-SPEECH*.

Aaron Jaech, Larry P. Heck, and Mari Ostendorf. 2016. Domain adaptation of recurrent neural networks for natural language understanding. In *INTERSPEECH*.

Rahul Jha, Alex Marin, Suvamsh Shivaprasad, and Imed Zitouni. 2018. Bag of experts architectures for model reuse in conversational language understanding. In *Proceedings of the 2018 Conference of the North American Chapter of the Association for Computational Linguistics: Human Language Technologies, Volume 3 (Industry Papers)*, volume 3, pages 153–161.

Yoon Kim, Yacine Jernite, David Sontag, and Alexander Rush. 2016. Character-aware neural language models. In *Proceedings of the 2016 Conference on Artificial Intelligence (AAAI)*.

Young-Bum Kim, Karl Stratos, and Dongchan Kim. 2017. Domain attention with an ensemble of experts. In *ACL*.

Young-Bum Kim, Karl Stratos, Ruhi Sarikaya, and Minwoo Jeong. 2015. New transfer learning techniques for disparate label sets. In *Proceedings of the 53rd Annual Meeting of the Association for Computational Linguistics and the 7th International Joint Conference on Natural Language Processing (Volume 1: Long Papers)*, volume 1, pages 473–482.

Diederik P Kingma and Jimmy Ba. 2014. Adam: A method for stochastic optimization. *arXiv preprint arXiv:1412.6980*.

Alexandros Komninos and Suresh Manandhar. 2016. Dependency based embeddings for sentence classification tasks. In *HLT-NAACL*.

Guillaume Lample, Miguel Ballesteros, Sandeep Subramanian, Kazuya Kawakami, and Chris Dyer. 2016. Neural architectures for named entity recognition. In *Proceedings of NAACL-HLT*, pages 260–270.

Jianhua Lin. 1991. Divergence measures based on the shannon entropy. *IEEE Transactions on Information theory*, 37(1):145–151.

Bing Liu and Ian Lane. 2016. Attention-based recurrent neural network models for joint intent detection and slot filling. In *Interspeech 2016*.

Bing Liu and Ian Lane. 2017a. Multi-Domain Adversarial Learning for Slot Filling in Spoken Language Understanding.

Bing Liu and Ian Lane. 2017b. Multi-domain adversarial learning for slot filling in spoken language understanding. In *NIPS Workshop on Conversational AI*.

Jingjing Liu, Panupong Pasupat, Yining Wang, Scott Cyphers, and James R. Glass. 2013. Query understanding enhanced by hierarchical parsing structures. In *2013 IEEE Workshop on Automatic Speech Recognition and Understanding, Olomouc, Czech Republic, December 8-12, 2013*, pages 72–77.

Xuezhe Ma and Eduard Hovy. 2016. End-to-end sequence labeling via bi-directional lstm-cnns-crf. In *Proceedings of the 54th Annual Meeting of the Association for Computational Linguistics (Volume 1: Long Papers)*, volume 1, pages 1064–1074.

Barbara Plank and Gertjan Van Noord. 2011. Effective measures of domain similarity for parsing. In *Proceedings of the 49th Annual Meeting of the Association for Computational Linguistics: Human Language Technologies-Volume 1*, pages 1566–1576. Association for Computational Linguistics.

Sameer Pradhan, Alessandro Moschitti, Nianwen Xue, Hwee Tou Ng, Anders Björkelund, Olga Uryupina, Yuchen Zhang, and Zhi Zhong. 2013. Towards robust linguistic analysis using ontonotes. In *Proceedings of the Seventeenth Conference on Computational Natural Language Learning*, pages 143–152.

Nils Reimers and Iryna Gurevych. 2017. Reporting Score Distributions Makes a Difference: Performance Study of LSTM-networks for Sequence Tagging. In *Proceedings of the 2017 Conference on Empirical Methods in Natural Language Processing (EMNLP)*, pages 338–348, Copenhagen, Denmark.

Sebastian Ruder and Barbara Plank. 2017a. Learning to select data for transfer learning with bayesian optimization. In *EMNLP*.

Sebastian Ruder and Barbara Plank. 2017b. Learning to select data for transfer learning with bayesian optimization. In *Proceedings of the 2017 Conference on Empirical Methods in Natural Language Processing*, pages 372–382, Copenhagen, Denmark. Association for Computational Linguistics.

Anders Søgaard and Yoav Goldberg. 2016. Deep multi-task learning with low level tasks supervised at lower layers. In *Proceedings of the 54th Annual Meeting of the Association for Computational Linguistics (Volume 2: Short Papers)*, volume 2, pages 231–235.

Erik F Tjong Kim Sang and Fien De Meulder. 2003. Introduction to the conll-2003 shared task: Language-independent named entity recognition. In *Proceedings of the seventh conference on Natural language learning at HLT-NAACL 2003-Volume 4*, pages 142–147. Association for Computational Linguistics.

Gökhan Tür, Dilek Z. Hakkani-Tür, and Larry P. Heck. 2010. What is left to be understood in atis? *2010 IEEE Spoken Language Technology Workshop*, pages 19–24.

Yu Wang, Yilin Shen, and Hongxia Jin. 2018. A bi model based rnn semantic frame parsing model for intent detection and slot filling. In *NAACL*.

Zhilin Yang, Ruslan Salakhutdinov, and William W Cohen. 2017. Transfer learning for sequence tagging with hierarchical recurrent networks. *arXiv preprint arXiv:1703.06345*.

Why are Sequence-to-Sequence Models So Dull?
Understanding the Low-Diversity Problem of Chatbots

Shaojie Jiang
University of Amsterdam
Amsterdam, The Netherlands
s.jiang@uva.nl

Maarten de Rijke
University of Amsterdam
Amsterdam, The Netherlands
m.derijke@uva.nl

Abstract

Diversity is a long-studied topic in information retrieval that usually refers to the requirement that retrieved results should be non-repetitive and cover different aspects. In a conversational setting, an additional dimension of diversity matters: an engaging response generation system should be able to output responses that are diverse and interesting. Sequence-to-sequence (Seq2Seq) models have been shown to be very effective for response generation. However, dialogue responses generated by Seq2Seq models tend to have low diversity. In this paper, we review known sources and existing approaches to this low-diversity problem. We also identify a source of low diversity that has been little studied so far, namely model over-confidence. We sketch several directions for tackling model over-confidence and, hence, the low-diversity problem, including confidence penalties and label smoothing.

1 Introduction

Sequence-to-sequence (Seq2Seq) models (Sutskever et al., 2014) have been designed for sequence learning. Generally, a Seq2Seq model consists of two recurrent neural networks (RNN) as its encoder and decoder, respectively, through which the model cannot only deal with inputs and outputs with variable lengths separately, but also be trained end-to-end. Seq2Seq models can use different settings for the encoder and decoder networks, such as the number of input/output units, ways of stacking layers, dictionary, etc. After showing promising results in machine translation (MT) tasks (Sutskever et al., 2014; Wu et al., 2016), Seq2Seq models also proved to be effective for tasks like question answering (Yin et al., 2015), dialogue response generation (Vinyals and Le, 2015), text summarization (Nallapati et al., 2016), constituency parsing (Vinyals et al., 2015a), image captioning (Vinyals et al., 2015b), and so on.

Seq2Seq models form the cornerstone of modern response generation models (Vinyals and Le, 2015; Li et al., 2015; Serban et al., 2016, 2017; Zhao et al., 2017). Although Seq2Seq models can generate grammatical and fluent responses, it has also been reported that the corpus-level diversity of Seq2Seq models is usually low, as many responses are trivial or non-committal, like "I don't know", "I'm sorry" or "I'm OK" (Vinyals and Le, 2015; Sordoni et al., 2015; Serban et al., 2016; Li et al., 2015). We refer to this problem as the *low-diversity* problem.

In recent years, there have been several types of approach to diagnosing and addressing the low-diversity problem. The purpose of this paper is to understand the low-diversity problem, to understand what diagnoses and solutions have been proposed so far, and to explore possible new approaches. We first review the theory of Seq2Seq models, then we give an overview of known causes and existing solutions to the low-diversity problem. We then connect the low-diversity problem to the concept of *model over-confidence*, and propose approaches to address the over-confidence problem and, hence, the low-diversity problem.

2 Sequence-to-Sequence Response Generation

Consider a dataset of message-response pairs (X, Y), where $X = (x_1, x_2, \ldots, x_{|X|})$ and $Y = (y_1, y_2, \ldots, y_{|Y|})$ are the input and output sequences, respectively. During training, the goal is to learn the relationships between X and Y, which can be formulated as maximizing the Seq2Seq model probability of Y given X:

$$\max p(Y|X) = \max \prod_{t=1}^{|Y|} p(y_t|y_{<t}, X), \quad (1)$$

where $y_{<t} = (y_1, y_2, \ldots, y_{t-1})$ are the ground-truth tokens of previous steps.

81

Proceedings of the 2018 EMNLP Workshop SCAI: The 2nd Int'l Workshop on Search-Oriented Conversational AI, pages 81–86
Brussels, Belgium, October 31, 2018. ©2018 Association for Computational Linguistics

Usually, Seq2Seq models employ Long Short-Term Memory (LSTM) networks as their encoder and decoder. The way a Seq2Seq models realizes (1), is to process the training inputs and outputs separately. On the encoder side, the input sequence X is encoded step-by-step, e.g., at step t:

$$h_t^{enc} = f_\theta^{enc}(h_{t-1}^{enc}, x_t), \qquad (2)$$

where $h_0^{enc} = \mathbf{0}$ is the initial hidden state of the encoder LSTM, and θ is the model parameter. The hidden state of the last step $h_{|X|}^{enc}$ is the vector representation of input sequence X.

Then, the decoder LSTM is initialized by $h_0^{dec} = h_{|X|}^{enc}$ so that output tokens can be based on the input:

$$h_t^{dec} = f_\theta^{dec}(h_{t-1}^{dec}, y_{t-1}), \qquad (3)$$

with y_0 as a special token (e.g., _START_) to indicate the decoder to start generation, and y_{t-1} as the ground truth token of the last time step. The hidden state h_t^{dec} is further used to predict the output distribution by using a multi-layer perceptron (MLP) and softmax function:

$$P(y_t|y_{<t}, X) = \frac{\exp(c_i f_\theta^{MLP}(h_t^{dec}))}{\sum_{j=1}^{N} \exp(c_j f_\theta^{MLP}(h_t^{dec}))}, \qquad (4)$$

where c_* are possible candidates of y_t, which are usually represented as word embeddings. After obtaining this distribution, we can calculate the loss compared with the ground-truth distribution by using, e.g., the cross-entropy loss function, and then we can back-propagate the loss to force the Seq2Seq model to maximize (1).

At test time at t, the step-wise decoder output distribution is conditioned on the actual model outputs $\hat{y}_{<t}$ and X, and the token with the highest probability is chosen as the output:

$$\hat{y}_t = \arg\max_{y_t} p(y_t|\hat{y}_{<t}, X), \qquad (5)$$

which is known as the maximum *a posteriori* (MAP) objective function.

3 Diagnosing the Low-Diversity Problem

In the literature, three dominant viewpoints on the low-diversity problem have been shared: lack of variability, improper objective function, and weak conditional signal. Below, we review these diagnoses of the low-diversity problem, with corresponding solutions, and we add a fourth diagnosis: model over-confidence.

3.1 Lack of variability

Serban et al. (2017); Zhao et al. (2017) trace the cause of the low-diversity problem in Seq2Seq models back to the lack of model variability. The variability of Seq2Seq models is different from that of retrieval-based chatbots (Fedorenko et al., 2017): in this study, we focus on the lack of variability of system responses, while in (Fedorenko et al., 2017), the authors deal with the low variability between responses and contexts.

To increase variability, Serban et al. (2017); Zhao et al. (2017) propose to introduce variational autoencoders (VAEs) to Seq2Seq models. At generation time, the latent variable z brought by a VAE is used as a conditional signal of the decoder LSTM (Serban et al., 2017):

$$h_t^{dec} = f_\theta^{dec}(h_{t-1}^{dec}, y_{t-1}, z), \qquad (6)$$

where we omit the contextual hidden states for simplicity.

At test time, z is *randomly* sampled from a prior distribution. Although being effective, the improvement in the degree of diversity of generated responses brought by this kind of method is actually brought by the randomness of z. The underlying Seq2Seq model remains sub-optimal in terms of diversity.

3.2 Improper objective function

Li et al. (2015) notice that the MAP objective function may be the cause of the low-diversity problem, since it can favor certain responses by only maximizing $p(Y|X)$. Therefore, they propose to maximize the mutual information between X, Y pairs:

$$\log \frac{p(X, Y)}{p(X)p(Y)}. \qquad (7)$$

With the help of Bayes' theorem, they derive two Maximum Mutual Information (MMI) objective functions:

$$\hat{Y} = \arg\max_{Y} \{ \log p(Y|X) - \\ \lambda \log p(Y) + \gamma|Y| \}, \qquad (8)$$

and

$$\hat{Y} = \arg\max_{Y} \{ (1-\lambda) \log p(Y|X) + \\ \lambda \log p(X|Y) + \gamma|Y| \}, \qquad (9)$$

where λ and γ are hyper-parameters. Here, $\log p(Y)$ and $\log p(X|Y)$ are the language model and a reverse model, respectively, with the latter trained using response-message pairs: (Y, X). Besides the time needed for training a reverse model, it should be noted that both objective functions need the length $|Y|$ of candidate responses, which are maintained in N-best lists generated by beam search. To obtain N-best lists with enough diversity, Li et al. (2015) use a beam size of 200 during testing, which is much more time-consuming than the basic Seq2Seq model.

Influenced by the MMI methods, several beam search based approaches (Li et al., 2016; Vijayakumar et al., 2016; Shao et al., 2017) focus on improving the diversity of N-best lists, in the hope of further enhancing the one-best response diversity. However, there are other faster approaches to the low-diversity problem without using beam search, such as the attention-based model that we describe below.

3.3 Weak conditional signal

Since attention layers (Bahdanau et al., 2014) have been introduced into Seq2Seq models for the MT task, they have also been a *de facto* standard module of Seq2Seq models for response generation. The purpose of Seq2Seq attention layers is different from the purpose of the Transformer model (Vaswani et al., 2017). Transformer proposes to rely only on self-attention and avoid using reccurence or convolutions, while attention layers of Seq2Seq aim at strengthening the input signal.

Although the introducing of attention layers can bring improvements to the response generation task, Tao et al. (2018) argue that the original attention signal often focuses on particular parts of the input sequence, which is not strong enough for the Seq2Seq model to generate specific responses, thus causing the low-diversity problem. The authors propose to use multiple attention heads to encourage the model to focus on various aspects of the input, by mapping encoder hidden states to K different semantic spaces:

$$h_{t,k}^{enc} = W_p^k \cdot h_t^{enc}, \tag{10}$$

where $W_p^k \in \mathbb{R}^{d \times d}$ is a learnable projection matrix. The net effect of the extended attention mechanism is, indeed, improvements in the diversity of generated responses. Readers are referred to (Tao et al., 2018) for more details.

3.4 Model over-confidence

As indicated by Hinton et al. (2015), one can think of the knowledge captured in conversation modeling as a mapping from input sequence X to output sequence Y, i.e., the distribution $P(Y|X)$. Therefore, if responses have a low degree of diversity, the learned distribution $P(Y|X)$ is questionable, as re-confirmed by Li et al. (2015). According to (1), the sequence-level distribution $P(Y|X)$ has a direct relationship with the token-level distribution. Therefore, we hypothesize that the token-level distribution $P(y_t|y_{<t}, X)$, produced at the decoder side, may be the culprit.

The decoder LSTM serves as an RNN language model (RNNLM) conditioned on the input sequence (Sutskever et al., 2014). With time steps increasing, the influence of the input sequence X will become weaker according to (3), and if the token-level distribution $P(y_t|y_{<t}, X)$ is problematic, it will have further effects on subsequent outputs (a "snowball effect"). An attention mechanism (Bahdanau et al., 2014; Tao et al., 2018) can be used to reinforce the influence of the input sequence, but there are still chances that the detrimental effect of $P(y_t|y_{<t}, X)$ is stronger than the input signal.

To analyze the problem of $P(y_t|y_{<t}, X)$, we train a Seq2Seq model[1] without attention layer, and plot the token-level distribution of generic responses in Figure 1. Interestingly, we find that the distributions shown signs of model over-confidence (Pereyra et al., 2017). When an attention mechanism is used, similar distributions can still be observed, as illustrated in Figure 2. From these two figures, we can see a common trend of growing confidence: the highest probabilities at each step keep growing, which confirms our conjecture of a snowball effect. Due to this effect, the final several tokens are of low quality, e.g., the no-attention model in Figure 1 starts to repeat itself, and the word "overlapping" in the attention model in Figure 2 is irrelevant for the user input.

A prediction is confident if the entropy of the output distribution is low. *Over-confidence* is often a symptom of over-fitting (Szegedy et al., 2016), which suggests that the inputs or outputs share much similarity from unknown aspects. Although it is hard to figure out what causes the over-fitting, maximizing entropy can usually help to regularize the model, making it generalize better. In (Pereyra et al., 2017), the authors propose to add the negative

---

[1] We are using ParlAI framework (Miller et al., 2017).

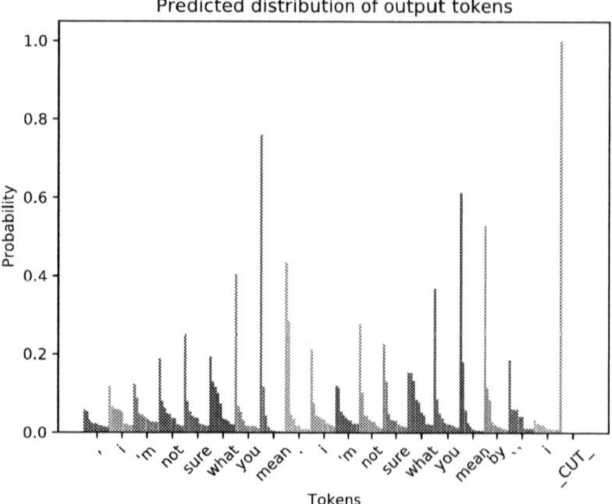

Figure 1: Given the input sequence: *how about we recognize the brilliance in everyone, or in mankind as a whole.*, the predicted distribution of model outputs, and tokens on x axis are MAP predictions. Note that we kept top-10 probabilities at each prediction step for simplicity and this output was cut before the _EOS_ token was emitted.

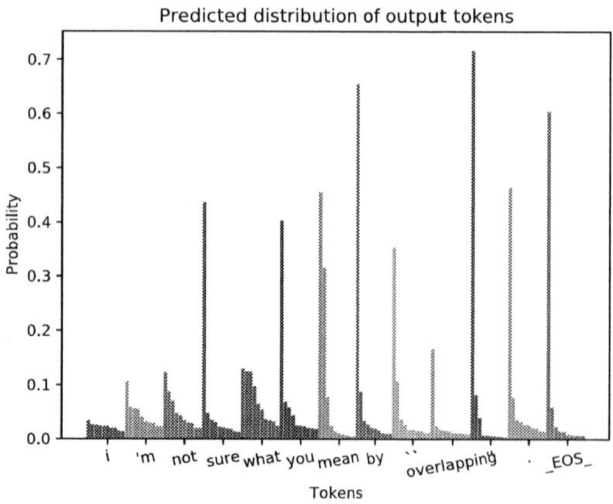

Figure 2: Predicted distribution of the same input as in Figure 1 when an attention mechanism is used.

entropy to the negative log-likelihood loss function during training, which can easily be tailored for conversation modeling:

$$\mathcal{L}(\theta) = -\sum_{i=1}^{N} \log p(c_i|y_{<t}, X) - \\ \beta H(p(c_i|y_{<t}, X)),$$

(11)

where β controls the strength of the confidence penalty, and $H(\cdot)$ is the entropy of the output dis-

tribution:

$$H(p(c_i|y_{<t}, X)) = \\ -\sum_{i=1}^{N} p(c_i|y_{<t}, X) \log(p(c_i|y_{<t}, X)).$$

(12)

The authors also show that this confidence penalty method is closely related to label smoothing regularization (Szegedy et al., 2016), therefore methods like neighborhood smoothing (Chorowski and Jaitly, 2016) may be used to solve the low-diversity problem.

So far, there has been no published work on analyzing the the effectiveness of correcting for model over-confidence on the low-diversity problem. It is important to note the fourth diagnosis of the low-diversity problem, i.e., that the problem is due to model over-confidence, is essentially different from the three types of diagnosis that we described earlier in the section. Among diagnoses and methods published previously, the VAE-based approaches actually bypass the low-diversity problem by introducing randomness; MMI-based methods have an elegant theoretical basis, yet they end up relying on many extra modules, like reverse models and beam search, and the newly-introduced hyper-parameters were not even learned from training data (Li et al., 2015); attention-based models offer a complementary approach, since strengthening the conditional signal is likely to make the response more specific, which should in turn improve the corpus-level diversity. Model over-confidence may offer a simpler alternative – we believe that methods such as confidence penalty are likely to alleviate the low-diversity problem in ways that differ from previous approaches.

4 Next Steps

In this paper, we described the low-diversity problem for response generation, which is one of the main issues faced by current Seq2Seq-based conversation models. We reviewed existing diagnoses and corresponding approaches to this problem and also added a diagnosis that has not been proposed or used so far, i.e., model over-confidence.

By using entropy maximizing approaches, such as confidence penalty (Pereyra et al., 2017) or label smoothing (Szegedy et al., 2016), we believe that the low-diversity problem of Seq2Seq models can be alleviated. Besides, by using entropy maximizing methods, the self-repeating problem

(Li et al., 2017) of Seq2Seq models may also be alleviated since this can reduce the snowball effect and make later outputs more relevant. We also noticed that the low-diversity problem resembles the mode collapse problem of GANs (Goodfellow et al., 2014), therefore inspirations may be drawn from the solutions like (Salimans et al., 2016; Metz et al., 2016).

In addition, since we now have four types of diagnosis of the low-diversity problem, each of which is likely to address part of the problem but not all of the problem, it is natural to systematically compare and combine approaches based on the different types of diagnosis. Understanding how solutions to the low-diversity problem helps to improve the effectiveness of conversational agents for search-oriented tasks is another interesting line of future work.

Acknowledgments

This research was supported by the China Scholarship Council.

References

Dzmitry Bahdanau, Kyunghyun Cho, and Yoshua Bengio. 2014. Neural machine translation by jointly learning to align and translate. *arXiv preprint arXiv:1409.0473*.

Jan Chorowski and Navdeep Jaitly. 2016. Towards better decoding and language model integration in sequence to sequence models. *arXiv preprint arXiv:1612.02695*.

Denis Fedorenko, Nikita Smetanin, and Artem Rodichev. 2017. Avoiding echo-responses in a retrieval-based conversation system. *arXiv preprint arXiv:1712.05626*.

Ian Goodfellow, Jean Pouget-Abadie, Mehdi Mirza, Bing Xu, David Warde-Farley, Sherjil Ozair, Aaron Courville, and Yoshua Bengio. 2014. Generative adversarial nets. In *Advances in neural information processing systems*, pages 2672–2680.

Geoffrey Hinton, Oriol Vinyals, and Jeff Dean. 2015. Distilling the knowledge in a neural network. *arXiv preprint arXiv:1503.02531*.

Jiwei Li, Michel Galley, Chris Brockett, Jianfeng Gao, and Bill Dolan. 2015. A diversity-promoting objective function for neural conversation models. *arXiv preprint arXiv:1510.03055*.

Jiwei Li, Will Monroe, and Dan Jurafsky. 2016. A simple, fast diverse decoding algorithm for neural generation. *arXiv preprint arXiv:1611.08562*.

Jiwei Li, Will Monroe, Tianlin Shi, Alan Ritter, and Dan Jurafsky. 2017. Adversarial learning for neural dialogue generation. *arXiv preprint arXiv:1701.06547*.

Luke Metz, Ben Poole, David Pfau, and Jascha Sohl-Dickstein. 2016. Unrolled generative adversarial networks. *arXiv preprint arXiv:1611.02163*.

Alexander H Miller, Will Feng, Adam Fisch, Jiasen Lu, Dhruv Batra, Antoine Bordes, Devi Parikh, and Jason Weston. 2017. Parlai: A dialog research software platform. *arXiv preprint arXiv:1705.06476*.

Ramesh Nallapati, Bowen Zhou, Caglar Gulcehre, Bing Xiang, et al. 2016. Abstractive text summarization using sequence-to-sequence rnns and beyond. *arXiv preprint arXiv:1602.06023*.

Gabriel Pereyra, George Tucker, Jan Chorowski, Łukasz Kaiser, and Geoffrey Hinton. 2017. Regularizing neural networks by penalizing confident output distributions. *arXiv preprint arXiv:1701.06548*.

Tim Salimans, Ian Goodfellow, Wojciech Zaremba, Vicki Cheung, Alec Radford, and Xi Chen. 2016. Improved techniques for training gans. In *Advances in Neural Information Processing Systems*, pages 2234–2242.

Iulian Vlad Serban, Alessandro Sordoni, Yoshua Bengio, Aaron C Courville, and Joelle Pineau. 2016. Building end-to-end dialogue systems using generative hierarchical neural network models. In *AAAI*, volume 16, pages 3776–3784.

Iulian Vlad Serban, Alessandro Sordoni, Ryan Lowe, Laurent Charlin, Joelle Pineau, Aaron C Courville, and Yoshua Bengio. 2017. A hierarchical latent variable encoder-decoder model for generating dialogues. In *AAAI*, pages 3295–3301.

Louis Shao, Stephan Gouws, Denny Britz, Anna Goldie, Brian Strope, and Ray Kurzweil. 2017. Generating high-quality and informative conversation responses with sequence-to-sequence models. *arXiv preprint arXiv:1701.03185*.

Alessandro Sordoni, Michel Galley, Michael Auli, Chris Brockett, Yangfeng Ji, Margaret Mitchell, Jian-Yun Nie, Jianfeng Gao, and Bill Dolan. 2015. A neural network approach to context-sensitive generation of conversational responses. *arXiv preprint arXiv:1506.06714*.

Ilya Sutskever, Oriol Vinyals, and Quoc V Le. 2014. Sequence to sequence learning with neural networks. In *Advances in neural information processing systems*, pages 3104–3112.

Christian Szegedy, Vincent Vanhoucke, Sergey Ioffe, Jon Shlens, and Zbigniew Wojna. 2016. Rethinking the inception architecture for computer vision. In *Proceedings of the IEEE conference on computer vision and pattern recognition*, pages 2818–2826.

Chongyang Tao, Shen Gao, Mingyue Shang, Wei Wu, Dongyan Zhao, and Rui Yan. 2018. Get the point of my utterance! learning towards effective responses with multi-head attention mechanism. In *IJCAI*, pages 4418–4424.

Ashish Vaswani, Noam Shazeer, Niki Parmar, Jakob Uszkoreit, Llion Jones, Aidan N Gomez, Łukasz Kaiser, and Illia Polosukhin. 2017. Attention is all you need. In *Advances in Neural Information Processing Systems*, pages 6000–6010.

Ashwin K Vijayakumar, Michael Cogswell, Ramprasath R Selvaraju, Qing Sun, Stefan Lee, David Crandall, and Dhruv Batra. 2016. Diverse beam search: Decoding diverse solutions from neural sequence models. *arXiv preprint arXiv:1610.02424*.

Oriol Vinyals, Łukasz Kaiser, Terry Koo, Slav Petrov, Ilya Sutskever, and Geoffrey Hinton. 2015a. Grammar as a foreign language. In *Advances in Neural Information Processing Systems*, pages 2773–2781.

Oriol Vinyals and Quoc Le. 2015. A neural conversational model. *arXiv preprint arXiv:1506.05869*.

Oriol Vinyals, Alexander Toshev, Samy Bengio, and Dumitru Erhan. 2015b. Show and tell: A neural image caption generator. In *Proceedings of the IEEE conference on computer vision and pattern recognition*, pages 3156–3164.

Yonghui Wu, Mike Schuster, Zhifeng Chen, Quoc V Le, Mohammad Norouzi, Wolfgang Macherey, Maxim Krikun, Yuan Cao, Qin Gao, Klaus Macherey, et al. 2016. Google's neural machine translation system: Bridging the gap between human and machine translation. *arXiv preprint arXiv:1609.08144*.

Jun Yin, Xin Jiang, Zhengdong Lu, Lifeng Shang, Hang Li, and Xiaoming Li. 2015. Neural generative question answering. *arXiv preprint arXiv:1512.01337*.

Tiancheng Zhao, Ran Zhao, and Maxine Eskenazi. 2017. Learning discourse-level diversity for neural dialog models using conditional variational autoencoders. *arXiv preprint arXiv:1703.10960*.

Retrieve and Refine:
Improved Sequence Generation Models For Dialogue

Jason Weston, Emily Dinan and Alexander H. Miller

Facebook AI Research

`jase@fb.com, edinan@fb.com, ahm@fb.com`

Abstract

Sequence generation models for dialogue are known to have several problems: they tend to produce short, generic sentences that are uninformative and unengaging. Retrieval models on the other hand can surface interesting responses, but are restricted to the given retrieval set leading to erroneous replies that cannot be tuned to the specific context. In this work we develop a model that combines the two approaches to avoid both their deficiencies: first retrieve a response and then refine it – the final sequence generator treating the retrieval as additional context. We show on the recent CON-VAI2 challenge task our approach produces responses superior to both standard retrieval and generation models in human evaluations.

1 Introduction

Sequence generation models like Seq2Seq (Sutskever et al., 2014) are increasingly popular for tasks such as machine translation (MT) and summarization, where generation is suitably constrained by the source sentence. However, obtaining good performance on dialogue tasks, where the context still allows many interpretations, remains an open problem despite much recent work (Serban et al., 2016). Several authors report the issue that they produce short, generic sentences containing frequent words – the so-called "I don't know" problem – as that response can work as a reply in many instances, but is uninformative and unengaging. Retrieval models (Ji et al., 2014) do not have this problem, but instead either produce engaging responses or else completely erroneous ones which they cannot

tune to the specific context, as they can only produce a valid reply if it is in the retrieval set.

In this work we propose a Retrieve and Refine model to gain the advantages of both methods, and avoid both their disadvantages. Models that produce an initial prediction and then refine it are growing in traction in NLP. They have been used in MT and summarization either for refinement of initial predictions (Junczys-Dowmunt and Grundkiewicz, 2017; Niehues et al., 2016; Novak et al., 2016; Xia et al., 2017; Grangier and Auli, 2017) or combining with retrieval (Gu et al., 2017; Cao et al., 2018), as well as for sentence correction or refinement without context (Guu et al., 2017; Schmaltz et al., 2017). There is little work in applying these methods to dialogue; one work we are aware of has been done concurrently with ours is Pandey et al. (2018). The usefulness of our approach is shown with detailed experiments on the ConvAI2 dataset[1] which is a chit-chat task to get to know the other speaker's profile, obtaining generations superior to both retrieval and sequence generation models in human evaluations.

2 Retrieve and Refine

The model we propose in this work is remarkably straight-forward: we take a standard generative model and concatenate the output of a retrieval model to its usual input, and then generate as usual, training the model under this setting.

For the generator, we use a standard Seq2Seq model: a 2-layer LSTM with attention. For the retriever, we use the Key-Value Memory Network (Miller et al., 2016) already shown to perform well for this dataset (Zhang et al., 2018), which attends over the dialogue history, to learn input and candidate retrieval embeddings that match using cosine similarity. The top scoring utterance is provided

Proceedings of the 2018 EMNLP Workshop SCAI: The 2nd International Workshop on Search-Oriented Conversational AI 978-1-948087-75-9

[1]`http://convai.io/`

87

Proceedings of the 2018 EMNLP Workshop SCAI: The 2nd Int'l Workshop on Search-Oriented Conversational AI, pages 87–92
Brussels, Belgium, October 31, 2018. ©2018 Association for Computational Linguistics

as input to our Seq2Seq model in order to refine it, prepended with a special separator token. For both models we use the code available in ParlAI[2]. At test time the retriever retrieves candidates from the training set.

To train our model we first precompute the retrieval result for every dialogue turn in the training set, but instead of using the top ranking results we rerank the top 100 predictions of each by their similarity to the label (in embedding space). Following Guu et al. (2017) this should help avoid the problem of the refinement being too far away from the original retrieval. We then append the chosen utterances to the input sequences used to train Seq2Seq. We refer to our model as *RetrieveN-Refine*, or *RetNRef* for short. We also consider two variants of the model in the following that we found improve the results.

Use Retriever More In our vanilla model, we noticed there was not enough attention being paid to the retrieval utterance by the generator. As the input to Seq2Seq is the dialogue history concatenated with the retrieval utterance, truncating the history is one way to pay more attention to the retrieval. In particular for the ConvAI2 dataset we clip the initial profile sentences at the start of the dialogue, forcing the model to more strongly rely on the retriever which still has them.[3] We refer to this modification as *RetrieveNRefine*[+].

Fix Retrieval Copy Errors Our model learns to sometimes ignore the retrieval (when it is bad), sometimes use it partially, and other times simply copy it. However, when it is mostly copied but only changes a word or two, we observed it made mistakes more often than not, leading to less meaningful utterances. We thus also consider a variant that exactly copies the retrieval if the model generates with large word overlap (we chose >60%). Otherwise, we leave the generation untouched.[4] We refer to this as *RetrieveNRefine*[++].

---

[2] http://parl.ai
[3] Architectural changes might also deal with this issue, e.g. treating the two inputs as independent sources to do attention over, but we take the simplest possible approach here.
[4] Other approaches might also help with this problem such as using an explicit copy mechanism or to use BPE tokenization (Fan et al., 2017), but we leave those for future work.

RetNRef Retrieval Method	PPL
None (Vanilla Seq2Seq)	31.4
Random label	32.0
Memory Network	31.8
True label's neighbor	25.9
True label	9.2

Table 1: Perplexity on the ConvAI2 task test set with different types of retriever for RetNRef, see text.

3   Experiments

We conduct experiments on the recent ConvAI2 challenge dataset which uses a modified version of the PersonaChat dataset (Zhang et al., 2018) (larger, and with different processing). The dataset consists of conversations between crowdworkers who were randomly paired and asked to act the part of a given persona (randomly assigned from 1155 possible personas, created by another set of workers), chat naturally, and get to know each other during the conversation. There are around 160,000 utterances in around 11,000 dialogues, with 2000 dialogues for validation and test, which use non-overlapping personas.

3.1   Automatic Evaluation and Analysis

Perplexity Dialogue is known to be notoriously hard to evaluate with automated metrics (Liu et al., 2016). In contrast to machine translation, there is much less constraint on the output with many valid answers with little word overlap, e.g. there are many answers to "what are you doing tonight?". Nevertheless many recent papers report perplexity results in addition to human judgments. For the retrieve and refine case, perplexity evaluation is particularly flawed: if the retrieval points the model to a response that is very different from (but equally valid as) the true response, the model might focus on refining that and get poor perplexity.

We therefore test our model by considering various types of retrieval methods: (i) the best performing existing retriever model, the Memory Network approach from Zhang et al. (2018) (retrieving from the training set), (ii) a retriever that returns a random utterance from the training set, (iii) the true label given in the test set, and (iv) the closest nearest neighbor from the training set utterances to the true label, as measured by the embedding space of the Memory Network retriever model. While (iii) and (iv) cannot be used in a deployed system as they are unknown, they can be

Method	Word cnt	Char cnt	Rare Word % <100	Rare Word % <1k
Seq2Seq	11.7	40.5	0.4%	5.8%
RetNRef	11.8	40.4	1.1%	6.9%
RetNRef$^+$	12.1	45.0	1.7%	10.1%
RetNRef^{++}	12.7	48.1	2.3%	10.9%
MemNet	13.1	54.5	4.0%	15.3%
Human	13.0	54.6	3.0%	11.5%

Table 2: Output sequence statistics for the methods. Seq2Seq generates shorter sentences with more common words than humans, which RetNRef alleviates.

Method	<30%	30-60%	60-80%	>80%
Seq2Seq	56%	34%	7%	3%
RetNRef	41%	38%	13%	8%
RetNRef$^+$	26%	20%	12%	42%
RetNRef^{++}	26%	20%	0%	53%

Table 3: Word overlap between retrieved and generated utterances in RetNRef, and between Seq2Seq and the Memory Network retriever (first row).

used as a sanity check: a useful retrieve and refine should improve perplexity if given these as input. We also compare to a standard Seq2Seq model, i.e. no retrieval.

The results are given in Table 1. They show that the RetNRef model can indeed improve perplexity with label neighbors or the label itself. However, surprisingly there is almost no difference between using no retrieval, random labels or our best retriever. The RetNRef^{++} model – that truncates the dialogue history and focuses more on the retrieval utterance – does even worse in terms of perplexity: 48.4 using the Memory Network retriever. However, poor perplexity does not mean human judgments of the generated sequences will not improve; in fact we will see that they do in the next section. How to automatically evaluate these kinds of models still remains an open problem.

Word Statistics Another way to measure the salience of a generation model is to compare it to human utterances in terms of word statistics. We analyze the word statistics of our models in Table 2. Seq2Seq models are known to produce short sentences with more common words than humans. The statistics on the ConvAI2 dataset bear this out, where the Seq2Seq model responses have lower word and character counts and use fewer rare words than the human responses. The RetNRef

model (using the Memory Network retriever, retrieving from the training set) makes some improvements in this regard, e.g. doubling the use of rare words (with frequency less than 100) and smaller gains for words with frequency less than 1000, but are still not close to human statistics. The RetNRef^{++} model which boosts the use of the retrieval does better in this regard, making the statistics much closer to human ones. Of course these metrics do not measure whether the utterances are semantically coherent, but it is encouraging to see a model using rare words as without this we believe it is hard for it to be engaging.

Table 3 compares the word overlap between retrieved and generated sentences in the RetNRef variants in order to measure if RetNRef is either ignoring the retriever, or else paying too much attention to and copying it. As comparison, the first row also shows the overlap between the retriever and vanilla Seq2Seq which does not retrieve at all. The results show that RetNRef^{++} has >80% word overlap with the retriever output around half (53%) of the time, whereas Seq2Seq and RetNRef very rarely overlap with the retriever (3% and 8% of the time respectively have >80% overlap). This shows that our improved model RetNRef^{++} does use the retriever, but can also generate novel content when it wants to, which a standard retriever cannot.

3.2 Evaluation by Human Judgement Scores

Following the protocol in Zhang et al. (2018), we asked humans to conduct short dialogues with our models (100 dialogues each of 10-20 turns, so 600 dialogues in total), and then measure the engagingness, consistency, and fluency (all scored out of 5) as well as to try to detect the persona that the model is using, given the choice between that and a random persona. Consistency measures the coherence of the dialogue, e.g. "I have a dog" followed by "I have no pets" is not consistent.

The results are given in Table 4. They show engagingness scores superior to Seq2Seq for all RetNRef variants, and with RetNRef^{++} slightly outperforming the retriever which it conditions on. Importantly however, it maintains this performance whilst still being able to generate text which a retrieval model cannot. It also performs well in the other metrics, although like the Memory Network model, it is weaker at using the persona than Seq2Seq. Seq2Seq is inferior to the

Method	Engagingness	Fluency	Consistency	Persona
Seq2Seq (PPL)	2.70(1.17)	3.50(1.37)	3.90(1.37)	0.90(0.29)
Seq2Seq (100 epochs)	2.76(1.15)	3.53(1.14)	3.84(1.38)	0.85(0.35)
Memory Network	3.66(1.26)	3.83(1.26)	3.61(1.36)	0.73(0.44)
RetrieveNRefine	2.94(1.26)	3.65(1.28)	3.72(1.32)	0.90(0.30)
RetrieveNRefine$^+$	3.50(1.33)	3.63(1.13)	3.55(1.33)	0.71(0.45)
RetrieveNRefine^{++}	3.80(1.18)	3.74(1.19)	3.80(1.40)	0.65(0.47)

Table 4: Human Evaluation scores for the models, scoring fluency, engagingness, consistency and persona detection, with standard deviation in parentheses. We consider engagingness to be the most important metric.

Comparison (A vs. B)	Win Rate	A Wins	B Wins	Tie	p-value
RetrieveNRefine^{++} vs. Memory Network	54.5%	340	284	572	0.027
RetrieveNRefine^{++} vs. Seq2Seq	53.7%	571	492	203	0.016
RetrieveNRefine^{++} (retrieved) vs. Seq2Seq	53.8%	290	249	87	
RetrieveNRefine^{++} (generated) vs. Seq2Seq	53.6%	281	243	116	
RetrieveNRefine$^+$ vs. Memory Network	51.63%	492	461	243	
RetrieveNRefine$^+$ vs. Human	30.13%	69	160	14	
Seq2Seq vs. Human	26.84%	62	169	22	

Table 5: A/B testing by humans comparing model pairs, reporting win rates for A over B (excluding ties).

Person 1	hey , george here . lets be friends	yeah. well, i wish you luck there. we bought a cute 2 story house.
Person 2	hi george , i'm regina . do you enjoy dance ?	nice , i don't think i have ever left ohio.
Seq2Seq	i do not but i do have a lot of time to dance	i am sorry. i am so scared of twins.
MemNet	hello george my name is pink	i am from mississippi . just moved back here from austin texas
RetNRef$^+$	i do. i enjoy dance.	i am from tennessee. just moved here from austin texas.

Person 1	drinking coffee? what time is it there?	thank you for that , you are what you believe ?
Person 2	830 pm haha my dad is a construction worker so he works really late nights	look energy isn't physical , only spiritual
Seq2Seq	i am a big guy so i can help you	i am not sure what that means
MemNet	yep . moonlight is amazing but northern light grab you too	do you do any sports ? swimming helps me keep my energy up.
RetNRef$^+$	oh wow, that is a long time	do you do any sports ? swimming helps me keep my energy up

Table 6: Example dialogues (left) where RetNRef outperforms MemNet, and (right) where RetNRef outperforms Seq2Seq – by either paying attention to the retriever or not. The first two rows are the previous two dialogue turns by Person 1 & 2, the following rows are the predictions for the next utterance of Person 1 by the various models.

Memory Network Retriever in terms of engagement, in line with previous results. We also tried overtraining the Seq2Seq for 100 epochs instead of early stopping by validation on perplexity as it may overfit training sentences and act more as a retriever, but this did not help.

Some example dialogues of the RetNRef^{++} model performing well (as scored by the evaluators) are shown in Tables 7 and 8. Longer sentences from the bot (person 2) with more nuanced entity information typically come from attending to the retriever, whereas the generator can also produce shorter replies independent of the retriever that fit the context well. There are still issues however, such as repeated phrases by the generator, and some tendency to copy the speaking partner's phrases that could be improved.

3.3 A/B Testing by Humans

To compute a statistically more meaningful test, and to evaluate models more clearly against each other, we also tested models by pairing them against each other (different to the protocol previously used for this dataset). We took human-human paired dialogues from the test set, up to a randomly chosen turn, and then computed the response of two rival models. The resulting dialogue history and the two choices are given to a third annotator to evaluate and asked which model is best; they can also choose "unsure". We collected over 1000 such examples, with each conversation being evaluated twice. The results are given in Table 5.

Persona 1	**Persona 2**
I am relatively tall.	I like to play baseball.
I like mexican food.	I love eating seafood.
I drive a subaru legacy.	I enjoy learning new languages.
My dog's name is Drunky.	I'm currently going for a marketing degree.
I can touch my toes with my nose.	I want to design ads in the future.

[PERSON 1:] I'm driving to the mexican place tonight for dinner, but my Subaru is at the rental shop.
[PERSON 2:] Yummy. I love mexican food, but I never eat vegetables
[PERSON 1:] Oh, I do, I think that's why i'm so tall!
[PERSON 2:] how tall are you? I do not... I enjoy studying languages.
[PERSON 1:] I'm 6 foot, a lot taller than my dog, Drunky.
[PERSON 2:] I am sorry to hear that. I want to be 6 foot tall.
[PERSON 1:] Do you have any talents? I can reach my toes using my nose.
[PERSON 2:] Cool! I listen to audiobooks and speak one asian language. you like sushi? I do.
[PERSON 1:] Oh sushi is my next favorite, after Mexican. What kind of car do you have?
[PERSON 2:] I have a Nissan Sentra. I love it.

Table 7: Example dialog between a human (Person 1) and the RetNRef^{++} model (Person 2). References to never eating vegetables, listening to audiobooks and speaking one asian language and owning a Nissan Sentra appeared in the conditioned retrieved sentences, improving the overall engaging quality of the dialogue.

Persona 1	**Persona 2**
I am a lacto-ovo vegetarian.	I have brown hair.
I like to hike.	I am Latina.
I have red hair.	My mother works for special needs clients..
My favorite drink is sprite.	I am a healer.
I have a pet parrot named Tasha.	I love my family.

[PERSON 1:] I dont know about you but I love sprite. Its my favorite.
[PERSON 2:] I like dr pepper a lot, but sprite is my second favorite.
[PERSON 1:] Sprites great! I take it with me every day on my hikes.
[PERSON 2:] I bet. I love to go to the water
[PERSON 1:] Ya that sounds like a great time. I go with my pet parrot Tasha when I go
[PERSON 2:] that is a good idea. I wish I had a parrot.
[PERSON 1:] Ya its fun. As a pet owner you learn to love animals; im even a lactoovo vegetarian now
[PERSON 2:] I love animals. I am vegan so I eat vegan food.
[PERSON 1:] Sounds like me :D im vegan, im ginger, and i love sprite
[PERSON 2:] I love animals. I am vegan so I eat a lot of it.

Table 8: Example dialog between a human (Person 1) and the RetNRef^{++} model (Person 2). References to Dr. Pepper and wishing to have a parrot appeared in the conditioned retrieved sentences, improving the overall engaging quality of the dialogue. There are still issues however, such as repeated phrases by the generator, failure to use the persona adequately, and some tendency to copy the speaking partner's phrases that could be improved.

RetrieveNRefine obtains statistically significant wins over the retriever Memory Network model and the generator Seq2Seq model using a binomial two-tailed test, with win rates ∼54%. Breaking down the wins between when RetNRef^{++} exactly copies the retrieval utterance vs. generates we see that it chooses them about equally, with wins about equal in both cases. This shows it can effectively learn when to choose the retrieval utterance (when it is good), and when to ignore it and generate instead (when it is bad). Table 6, which shows example outputs of our model, illustrates this.

RetNRef^{+} sometimes loses out when making small changes to the retrieved text, for example it made changes to "i once broke my nose trying to peak in on a jazz concert !" by replacing

peak with *glacier*. Recall that RetNRef^{++} fixes this problem by exactly copying the retrieved text when there is insignificant word overlap with the generated text; as such, it has a correspondingly larger win rate against Memory Networks (54.5% versus 51.63%).

We also computed a small sample of A/B tests directly against humans rather than models, and again see the win rate is higher for RetNRef.

4   Conclusion

In conclusion, we showed that retrieval models can be successfully used to improve generation models in dialogue, helping them avoid common issues such as producing short sentences with frequent words that ultimately are not engaging. Our

RetNRef^{++} model has similar statistics to human utterances and provides more engaging conversations according to human judgments.

Future work should investigate improved ways to incorporate retrieval in generation, both avoiding the heuristics we used here to improve performance, and seeing if more sophisticated approaches than concatenation plus attention improve the results, for example by more clearly treating the inputs as independent sources, or training the models jointly.

References

Ziqiang Cao, Wenjie Li, Sujian Li, and Furu Wei. 2018. Retrieve, rerank and rewrite: Soft template based neural summarization. In *Proceedings of the 56th Annual Meeting of the Association for Computational Linguistics (Volume 1: Long Papers)*, volume 1, pages 152–161.

Angela Fan, David Grangier, and Michael Auli. 2017. Controllable abstractive summarization. *arXiv preprint arXiv:1711.05217*.

David Grangier and Michael Auli. 2017. Quickedit: Editing text & translations via simple delete actions. *arXiv preprint arXiv:1711.04805*.

Jiatao Gu, Yong Wang, Kyunghyun Cho, and Victor OK Li. 2017. Search engine guided nonparametric neural machine translation. *arXiv preprint arXiv:1705.07267*.

Kelvin Guu, Tatsunori B Hashimoto, Yonatan Oren, and Percy Liang. 2017. Generating sentences by editing prototypes. *arXiv preprint arXiv:1709.08878*.

Zongcheng Ji, Zhengdong Lu, and Hang Li. 2014. An information retrieval approach to short text conversation. *arXiv preprint arXiv:1408.6988*.

Marcin Junczys-Dowmunt and Roman Grundkiewicz. 2017. An exploration of neural sequence-to-sequence architectures for automatic post-editing. *arXiv preprint arXiv:1706.04138*.

Chia-Wei Liu, Ryan Lowe, Iulian V Serban, Michael Noseworthy, Laurent Charlin, and Joelle Pineau. 2016. How not to evaluate your dialogue system: An empirical study of unsupervised evaluation metrics for dialogue response generation. *arXiv preprint arXiv:1603.08023*.

Alexander Miller, Adam Fisch, Jesse Dodge, Amir-Hossein Karimi, Antoine Bordes, and Jason Weston. 2016. Key-value memory networks for directly reading documents. *arXiv preprint arXiv:1606.03126*.

Jan Niehues, Eunah Cho, Thanh-Le Ha, and Alex Waibel. 2016. Pre-translation for neural machine translation. *arXiv preprint arXiv:1610.05243*.

Roman Novak, Michael Auli, and David Grangier. 2016. Iterative refinement for machine translation. *arXiv preprint arXiv:1610.06602*.

Gaurav Pandey, Danish Contractor, Vineet Kumar, and Sachindra Joshi. 2018. Exemplar encoder-decoder for neural conversation generation. In *Proceedings of the 56th Annual Meeting of the Association for Computational Linguistics (Volume 1: Long Papers)*, volume 1, pages 1329–1338.

Allen Schmaltz, Yoon Kim, Alexander M Rush, and Stuart M Shieber. 2017. Adapting sequence models for sentence correction. *arXiv preprint arXiv:1707.09067*.

Iulian Vlad Serban, Ryan Lowe, Laurent Charlin, and Joelle Pineau. 2016. Generative deep neural networks for dialogue: A short review. *arXiv preprint arXiv:1611.06216*.

Ilya Sutskever, Oriol Vinyals, and Quoc V Le. 2014. Sequence to sequence learning with neural networks. In *Advances in neural information processing systems*, pages 3104–3112.

Yingce Xia, Fei Tian, Lijun Wu, Jianxin Lin, Tao Qin, Nenghai Yu, and Tie-Yan Liu. 2017. Deliberation networks: Sequence generation beyond one-pass decoding. In *Advances in Neural Information Processing Systems*, pages 1782–1792.

Saizheng Zhang, Emily Dinan, Jack Urbanek, Arthur Szlam, Douwe Kiela, and Jason Weston. 2018. Personalizing dialogue agents: I have a dog, do you have pets too? *arXiv preprint arXiv:1801.07243*.

Author Index